CHANNEL DEVELOPMENT & MANAGEMENT IN THE SOFTWARE INDUSTRY.

Building Successful Partner Channels

Hans Peter Bech

TBK Publishing® (an activity of TBK Consult Holding ApS)
Strandvejen 724
2930 Klampenborg
Denmark
CVR: DK31935741
www.tbkpublishing.com

ISBN 978-87-93116-16-0 (printed version)

When Microsoft acquired Navision in 2002 there is no doubt that the price they paid was heavily influenced by the value of our channel partner ecosystem. I can think of no one better suited than Hans Peter to write a book with the title Building Successful Partner Channels.

Preben Damgaard, Co-founder
and CEO of Navision

"Predictable growth and market leadership through independent channel partners are on every software industry CEO and sales executives' mind. However, it is rarely achieved. With "Building Successful Partner Channels" Hans Peter Bech provides a great tactical approach toward reaching this goal."

Torulf Nilsson, Product Executive,
Visma Retail, Oslo, Norway

"Hans Peter Bech has been at the forefront developing indirect channels in the software industry for more than three decades and his track record is impressive. I'd highly recommend this book to anyone searching for the route to global market leadership in the software industry."

Yusuf Soner, School of Management at the
Sabanci University, Istanbul, Turkey

"Building Successful Partner Channels provides a powerful, practical approach to building a strong network of independent channel partners, so as to optimize sales and marketing activities. The book helps senior sales and marketing executives understand how to work in concert to achieve global market leadership through the indirect-channel approach."

Toke Kruse, Founder and CEO at Billy,
San Francisco, USA

In memory of Gianmaria Odello

FOREWORD BY PREBEN DAMGAARD

When Microsoft acquired Navision in 2002 there is no doubt that the price they paid was heavily influenced by the value of our channel partner eco-system. As you may know, the Navision that Microsoft acquired was a company formed by the merger of Navision Software and Damgaard Data in 2000, the latter a company started by my brother and I in 1983.

From the very first day both Navision Software and Damgaard Data decided to take an indirect route to market and although our first generation products were not designed with the channel partner in mind, both companies released partner enabled products in the late 1980's. Navision (now Dynamics NAV), Concorde XAL (now Dynamics XAL) and AXAPTA (now Dynamics AX) were all designed as international products allowing the channel partners to extend the functionality, integrate to other products, perform customizations and deliver all sorts of product associated services. These concepts accelerated the proliferation of value-added products and services developed by our channel partners and created an eco-system reaching into corners of the market that we would never have dreamed of serving. The Navision and Damgaard eco-systems became the basis for many new and successful companies that employed thousands of people delivering value to thousands of customers all over the world.

Our journey from young start-ups to mature companies took place in a period of substantial change with trends that were very hard to predict and we constantly had to adjust our strategies and change our decisions when our expectations for the future proved to be inaccurate. Figuring out how to grow and manage the channel was something we had to learn along the way and it was by no means a straight road from A to B.

There is still no handbook for how to build channels in the software industry and I therefore welcome Hans Peter's initiative in documenting his experience and insight with channel partner eco-systems in this book. Providing general guidelines for channel building and management in the software industry is not an easy task given the rapidly growing diversity of products and markets and the enormous changes in technology and environment that are dramatically different compared to when we started out. Using the Osterwalder business model framework and drawing on his vast experience, Hans Peter manages to spell out the generic principles that apply in all situations at all times as well as discussing the possible impact of the changes we are currently witnessing in technology, communication and social media.

I first met Hans Peter in 1991 when he was country manager for Data General in Denmark and wanted Concorde XAL to be made available on their new AViiON series of UNIX computers. In 1997 Hans Peter joined Damgaard Data as part of the team designated to take over the international distribution from IBM and in early 1998 he moved to Germany and became responsible for our operations in the German speaking countries. In 1998 we also launched AXAPTA and Hans Peter was on the executive launch team participating in the development of all our partner programs for this product line. I can think of no one better suited than Hans Peter to write a book with the title Building Successful Partner Channels and I am sure you will find guidelines and inspiration that you can use directly in your own business.

Preben Damgaard
Copenhagen, March 2015

ACKNOWLEDGEMENT

The idea for writing this book comes from a series of workshops that I conducted for the Executive Development Unit of the Sabanci University in Istanbul, Turkey in Spring 2013. The workshops were an activity in the Turkish Government's UR-GE sectorial program for industrial development organized by IMMIB[1] for the software clusters companies in the "TETSoft Project" and sponsored by the Ministry of Economy. I developed a series of whitepapers for the workshops and was urged by IMMIB to document the entire content of the workshops in a book format. This book entitled Building Successful Partner Channels in the Software Industry is the first of two books, with the next being entitled Entering Foreign Markets in the Software Industry and is planned for publication in 2016.

The drafts have been thoroughly reviewed and commented on by a team of subject matter experts including Mohammad Adi, Regional Sales Manager at SEDCO in Jordan; Dick Bryer, President of Sales Builder Inc., Toronto, Canada; Pamela Campagna, principal at BLUE SAGE Consulting, Inc., Boston, Massachusetts, USA; Bjørn Eilertsen, Vice President with Milestone Systems A/S, Copenhagen, Denmark; Amit Gavankar, Regional Sales Manager with LeadSquared, Mumbai, Maharashtra, India; Fikret Idil, Executive Partner with TBK Consult in Istanbul, Turkey; Frank Meijer, Program Manager with VanMeijel Automatisering, Zwolle, The Netherlands; Torulf Nilsson, Product Executive with Visma Retail, Oslo, Norway; Gianmaria Odello, Executive Partner with TBK Consult in Milan, Italy; Per Steen Pedersen, principal at SMP

---

[1] Istanbul Minerals & Metals Exporters' Associations

Management, Copenhagen, Denmark; Bob Snyder, Editor-in-Chief with Channel Media Europe Ltd., Brussels, Belgium; Paul Solski, principal at AIM International, Seattle, State of Washington, USA. Without the numerous suggestions and recommendations from this team of experienced channel developers, the book would have been very different and would have missed some crucial issues and trends.

My dedicated PA Emma Crabtree has undertaken the editorial proofing from her residence in Condeixa-a-Velha, Portugal and the illustrations, book cover and layout come from the hand of Jelena Galkina with the design studio Sordako Oü in Tallinn, Estonia.

Hans Peter Bech
Hillerød, March 2015

TABLE OF CONTENTS:

FOREWORD BY PREBEN DAMGAARD _____ 7

ACKNOWLEDGEMENTS _____ 9

CHAPTER 1 _____ 15

INTRODUCTION _____ 15

WHO IS THIS BOOK WRITTEN FOR? _____ 15

WHAT IS YOUR SITUATION? _____ 17

DEFINITION OF BUSINESS MODEL AND

ENVIRONMENT CHARACTERISTICS _____ 18

WHAT IS A SOFTWARE COMPANY? _____ 20

WHAT IS A CHANNEL PARTNER? _____ 21

WHY THIS BOOK? _____ 22

HOW MANY PARTNERS DO WE NEED? _____ 24

CHAPTER 2 _____ 27

BOOK SUMMARY _____ 27

CHAPTER 3 _____ 31

CONCEPTUAL FRAMEWORK _____ 31

THE TWO PERSPECTIVES _____ 32
THE INTERNAL PERSPECTIVE
THE EXTERNAL PERSPECTIVE

THE BUSINESS MODEL _____ 34

THE CHANNEL _____ 35

CHAPTER 4 _____ 41

WHEN TO TAKE A CHANNEL ROUTE AND WHEN NOT TO TAKE THE

CHANNEL ROUTE? _____ 41
LOW (OR NO) TOUCH
MEDIUM TOUCH
HIGH TOUCH

NO OR LOW TOUCH _____ 43

MEDIUM TOUCH _____ 45

HIGH TOUCH _____ 46

CHAPTER 5 _____ 49

THE CHANEL PARTNER PROGRAM _____ 49

THE BUSINESS PARTNER AGREEMENT _____ 49

THE OBJECTIVE OF THE CHANNEL PARTNER PROGRAM _____ 51
SUPPORTING THE VALUE CHAIN
THE CHANNEL PARTNER PROGRAM AS A RECRUITMENT TOOL
STRATEGY WORKSHOP
THE PARTNER P&L
CERTIFICATION
TRAINING
MARKETING AND SALES INCENTIVES AND REPORTING

SUPPORT _____ 67
LEVELS OF SUPPORT
THE SUPPORT SYSTEM
THE KNOWLEDGE BASE

PRODUCT MANAGEMENT _____ 69

ONGOING CHANNEL PARTNER MANAGEMENT _____ 70

INCENTIVES _____ 71
PRODUCT MARGIN
MARKETING DEVELOPMENT FUNDING (MDF)
SALES PERFORMANCE INCENTIVE FUND (SPIF)
FUNDED HEADS
PLATINUM, GOLD AND SILVER

BUSINESS DEVELOPMENT _____ 74

THE CHANNEL PARTNER PORTAL _____ 74

CHANNEL PARTNER EVENTS _____ 75

CHAPTER 6 _____ 79

CHANNEL PARTNER RECRUITMENT _____ 79

DEFINING THE IDEAL PARTNER PROFILE _____ 80
DEMOGRAPHIC PROPERTIES
SOCIOGRAPHIC PROPERTIES
PSYCHOGRAPHIC PROPERTIES

COMPETITORS AND OUTLIERS _____ 83

THE CHANNEL PARTNER RECRUITMENT PROCESS _____ 83

THE SHORT-LIST _____ 85

Non-core Markets _____ 87
The Changing Dynamics of Channel Partner Recruitment____87
International Channel Partner Recruitment _____ 88
The Average Recruitment Cycle _____ 90
Strategic Channel Partner Recruitment _____ 91

Chapter 7 _____ 93
Channel Partner Management _____ 93
The Stars _____ 94
The Growth Potential _____ 96
The Rest _____ 96
The Partner Relationship Management System _____ 96
Partner Account Managers _____ 97

Chapter 8 _____ 99
Switching from Direct to Indirect _____ 99
Step One - Splitting our Company in Two _____ 100
Step Two - Building the "Distribution" Muscle _____ 101

Chapter 9 _____ 103
Channel Conflicts _____ 103
From Direct to Indirect _____ 103
From Indirect to Direct _____ 104
White Label and "OEM" channels _____ 104
Over-Penetration is Not a Channel Conflict _____ 105

Chapter 10 _____ 107
Distribution _____ 107
Tiers in the Channel Structure _____ 108
International Distribution _____ 110
Subsidiaries _____ 112
Value Added Distributors _____ 113

Chapter 11 _____ 115

SOFTWARE AS A SERVICE _____ 115
SOFTWARE SHOULD BE FREE OF CHARGE _____ 115
SIMPLICITY DEFEATS COMPLEXITY _____ 116
MOBILE _____ 117
PAY AS WE GO GIVES FULL INSIGHT _____ 118
CASHFLOW _____ 118
CUSTOMIZATION AND INTEGRATION _____ 119
MARGINS AND CUSTOMER RELATIONSHIPS _____ 120
INCUMBENTS AND INSURGENTS _____ 120

Appendices _____ 123

APPENDIX A _____ 125
CHANNEL PARTNER TYPES

APPENDIX B _____ 139
THE BUSINESS MODEL
VALUE PROPOSITIONS
THE BUSINESS MODEL ENVIRONMENT

APPENDIX C _____ 173
SAMPLE BUSINESS PARTNER AGREEMENT

APPENDIX D _____ 195
THE CHANNEL PARTNER P&L

APPENDIX E _____ 201
SOCIAL MEDIA MARKETING AND SALES:
POETS, PLUMBERS AND THE DEATH OF PROPAGANDA

APPENDIX F _____ 209
EXCLUSIVITY

APPENDIX G _____ 213
LITERATURE

Appendix H _____ 217

About the Author _____ 219

CHAPTER 1

INTRODUCTION

Welcome to my book about how to become a global market leader through independent channel partners. In this introductory chapter I will take you through some fundamental questions that I am always asked by my consulting clients when I run my workshops and that I also regularly receive in my mailbox based on my on-going writing on the subject.

Any book needs to choose between the pronoun "he" or "she." I flipped a coin and "she" won." Throughout the book I will use "she" and "her" instead of "he" and "his."
Let's get started.

WHO IS THIS BOOK WRITTEN FOR?

I have written this book for B2B[2] software industry executives[3] and their operational staff with companies that have chosen or are considering taking the indirect channel route to market leadership.

Is the ambition of achieving market leadership then a prerequisite for reading the book? No, it is not.

It is, however, a prerequisite for being successful in the software

---

[2] B2B: business-to-business.

[3] Thus I am referring to the software vendor, the principal, when I use the pronouns "we" and "us" in this book.

industry. The market leadership[4] ambition is even more important when we consider a go-to-market approach through independent channel partners. If we do not have the ambition of achieving market leadership in our industry then I cannot recommend the indirect channel approach because it will not work.

This statement is based on my 35 years + of personal operational experience, but it is also supported by common sense.

Channel partners want to work with the market leaders and not with unknown brands.

When channel partners choose to engage with an unknown software vendor they do so anticipating that they are joining a winning team for the future. By joining early they can enjoy surfing the steadily growing waves as the software vendor builds her brand, becomes recognized and market demand shifts from being push-driven[5] to becoming pull-driven[6].

Tell a channel partner that we have no ambitions of "making it big" and see what their reactions are. Channel partners are not interested in doing business with software companies that lack market leadership ambitions, because that may leave them in a cost-inefficient push-driven position forever.

---

[4] Successful companies strive to become number one or two in the (global) markets where they operate. As the software industry is young, extremely dynamic and mostly unconsolidated it can be hard to define exactly what market leadership means. However, if a company is not on the path to pass the 20% market share in their domestic market then they are most likely not on the path to becoming market leaders. The 20% is the "tipping point" (see Gladwell, Malcolm. 2002. The tipping point : how little things can make a big difference (Back Bay Books: Boston). and Moore, Geoffrey A. 2014. Crossing the chasm : marketing and selling disruptive products to mainstream customers (HarperBusiness, an imprint of HarperCollins Publishers: New York, NY). When passing the tipping point market forces kick in and accelerate demand for a product lowering the Customer Acquisition Cost and increases gross margin per unit sold.

[5] You will have to find potential customers and activate the need for your solution.

[6] The customers with an active need for the solution will find you.

Thus, the primary objective of this book is not just to discuss how to build a channel. The objective is to discuss how to become the global[7] market leader, if we have chosen to take the journey through independent channel partners.

The objective is market leadership.

The channel is "just" one of the means of getting and staying there.

WHAT IS YOUR SITUATION?

My fellow countryman Søren Kierkegaard said the following about education:

> *"... if real success is to attend the effort to bring a man to a definite position, one must first of all take pains to find him where he is and begin there[8]."*

The challenges you may face building and managing independent channel partners will differ substantially depending on the nature of your business model, its environment and your current situation.

Have you just started? Are you well under way? Do you want to switch from a direct to an indirect approach? Do you already run an indirect approach, but are having challenges? Do you have a standard or a platform product? Do you have short or long sales cycles? Etc.

As software companies can be very different animals I will introduce a set of characteristics that I will refer to throughout this book discussing the conditions that apply for the stages we are in and situations that we may be facing. In table 1 below I have chosen seven fundamental characteristics of business models, business model environments and channel development stages in the software industry.

---

[7] The software industry is with very few exceptions global by nature. Most software products requires no or only very little localization to travel across borders and even the products that do require substantial localization enjoy the economy of scale opportunities provided by the global market.

[8] Søren Kierkegaard, The Journals, 1854

DEFINITION OF BUSINESS MODEL AND ENVIRONMENT CHARACTERISTICS

Variable	Level 1	Level 2	Level 3
Company Matureness	**Start-up** Looking for a profitable and scalable business model	**Stable Growth** Profitable and growing faster than the market	**Leadership** Domestic market share >20% and global market penetration initiated
Market Matureness	**Emerging Market** There are only few and small providers of this type of solutions	**Fragmented Market** Several providers of thus type of solution, but non with >20% market share	**Mature Market** A few clear market leaders with < 20% market share
Channel Matureness	**Low** Less then 25% of the market can be reached through channel partners	**Medium** 25-50% of the market can be reached through channel partners	**High** >50% of the market can be reached through channel partners
Customer Touch and Sales Cycle	**Low** No field sales required -avg. sales cycles <3 months	**Medium** Field sales required-avg. sales cycles are <12 months	**High** Field sales required-avg. sales cycles are >12 months
Value-add Potential	**Low** Auxiliary products and services are <50% of CLV	**Medium** Auxiliary products and services are 50-75% of CLV	**High** Auxiliary products and services are >75% of CLV
Channel Importance	**Low** <25% of the revenue is from channel partners	**Medium** 25-50% of the revenue is from channel partners	**High** >50% of the revenue is from channel partners
Channel Development Stage	**Early Mode** <25% of the revenue is from current partners	**Growth Mode** 25-75% of the revenue is from current partners	**Mature Mode** 25-75% of the revenue is from current partners

Note: CLV=Customer Lifetime Value

This book is primarily written for software companies with a maturity Level 2 or 3, penetrating markets with a maturity Level 2 or 3, where there is an independent channel at a maturity Level 2 or 3, where the customer touch levels[9] and sales cycles are Level 2 or 3, where the value-add potential is Level 2 or 3 and with a channel importance Level 3. All of the general frameworks described in this book will work for all levels of channels development stages, but whenever I make a statement or provide a rule of thumb I have software companies with Level 2-3 type maturity in mind.

If you are switching from a direct go-to-market approach to an indirect go-to-market approach then this book is definitely for you although your current situation may not match with all the Level 2-3 scenarios in figure 1.

Please let me stress that the book is deliberately not written specifically for start-ups. However, I do realize that many start-ups are pondering exactly this question: direct or indirect? I have been in this very situation myself several times. In some situations we chose the indirect channel approach and became successful, but not without substantial homework and business model re-engineering along the way. In other situations we chose the direct approach and also became successful. And in some situations we failed irrespective of which approach we took.

I believe a start-up can take away value from reading this book, because the channel considerations should be an integrated part of defining and developing the value proposition. However, as a start-up we always need direct feedback from our ultimate customers. We cannot rely on only getting filtered market feedback through independent channel partners. If you are a start-up then I recommend you read Steve Blank's[10] books too, as he focuses entirely on start-ups.

---

[9] Customer Touch Levels - Please refer to Chapter 4 for more details.

[10] Blank, Steve; Dorf, Bob. 2012. The Startup Owner's Manual: The Step-By-Step Guide for Building a Great Company (K & S Ranch). www.steveblank.com

There are two measurements that I will use throughout this book as they will become increasingly critical in our rapidly changing environment[11] and have a fundamental impact on how to build and manage indirect partner channels:

Customer Acquisition Cost (CAC) is the total cost (marketing, sales and pre-sales) of acquiring a new customer. ACAC is the average customer acquisition cost.

Customer Lifetime Value (CLV) is the gross margin we can expect from a customer over the lifetime of our relationship. ACLV is the average customer lifetime value.

As the software industry is moving (rapidly?) from the prepaid perpetual license model to the recurring subscription model, careful management of ACAC and ACLV will be the key to survival and prosperity. If you are unfamiliar with these changes I suggest you start with reading chapter 11 before continuing with the rest of the book.

WHAT IS A SOFTWARE COMPANY?

You may ask: What is a software company?

I have included a discussion on this subject in Appendix A and will provide only the conclusion here:

> *In this book a software company is any company providing a B2B product and service where software is a major component irrespective of whether it is bundled with hardware, delivered as a perpetual, upfront paid, on-site license or delivered as a*

---

[11] A thorough analysis of the disruptive changes currently taking place in the software industry can be found in Wood, J. B., Todd Hewlin, and Thomas E. Lah. 2011. Consumption economics : the new rules of tech (Point B Inc.: California).

service through a browser or an app. The principles presented in this book are universal for B2B software based products and services irrespective of the delivery format.

WHAT IS A CHANNEL PARTNER?

Let's assume that we run a software company.

To run our business we need to find, win, make, keep and grow happy customers[12]. To grow our business we need to keep scaling and improving the productivity of the ways that we find, win, make, keep and grow happy customers. We can do so by hiring a steadily increasing number of sales and support staff, or we can convince someone else that they should find, win, make, keep and grow happy customers for our product.

We typically call that "someone else" an independent channel partner. We - the software company with the IP rights - then becomes the "principal."

Independent channel partners operate in their own name, at their own expense and at their own risk.

We are dealing at arms length with our independent channel partners[13].

Later in the book, I will also introduce the distributor[14] role, but for now we will focus on the principal and her resellers. Channel

---

[12] This is a generic representation of the sales process. Specific companies will have variations of this process such as find, try, buy/win, use, renew and grow/expand.

[13] Throughout this book I use the term "channel partner" and "reseller" synonymously.

[14] In the terminology of this book a distributor is serving independent channel partners on behalf of the vendor. We call a business model where the vendor is dealing directly with the independent channel partners a "1-tier" channel approach, while the use of distributors is called a "2-tier" channel approach.

partnerships in the software industry take many forms and shapes[15] and I have included a description of the most commonly used in Appendix A, too.

WHY THIS BOOK?

Using a channel of independent companies to find, win, make, keep and grow happy customers has a long tradition in the short history[16] of the software industry. For some software companies the channel has been a major contributor to global success, but for most software companies making it work remains a depressing and constant struggle.

Building indirect channels may be complicated, but it is not really that difficult. It is complicated because it requires an additional and completely different layer of business principles compared to the situation where we serve our customers directly. I believe this is the core of the trouble many software industry executives face when setting out to build a network of independent channel partners (that are supposed to find, win, make, keep and grow happy customers on their behalf). Software executives often grossly underestimate what it takes to recruit, enable and manage independent channel partners. Many software executives consider the independent channel partners as a readily available, flexible and inexpensive sales resource and nothing could be further from the truth. I hope that by sharing my experience and insight through this book that more software executives will make better decisions concerning their channel strategies and their subsequent implementation, helping them on the route to market leadership.

---

[15] A description of the most important types of partnerships is included in Appendix A.

[16] The software industry emerged with the personal computer (Apple and IBM) in the beginning of the 1980's. With the proliferation of the Internet from the beginning of the 1990's and the availability of smart mobile devices lead by the iPhone in 2007 the software industry has become a gigantic industry serving consumers and businesses of all types and sizes.

I started building independent channel partner networks in 1986. Coming from a small domestic market[17] I was forced to build *international* channel partner networks very early in the lifecycle of the companies where I was responsible for revenue generation and I also had to do it with very limited resources. I learned that you do not have to be big to be smart. Even small software companies can build powerful independent channel partner networks over time if they understand some fundamental business principles.

From 1997 to 2001 I was responsible for Damgaard's[18] activities in the German speaking markets and in this capacity I had the unique experience of introducing and building the channel for AXAPTA[19] in Germany, Austria and Switzerland. After the merger with Navision I was made responsible for our joint operations in Central Europe.

I left Navision in 2001 to start my own business and in 2003 I acquired a major share of a Microsoft Dynamics AX reseller[20] and held the position as CEO of the company. In this capacity I had intimate insight into the daily life of a value added reseller of a product that I was previously responsible for launching to independent channel partners in the German speaking markets. Having served on both sides of the table helped me to deepen my understanding of the principal/partner relationship and the completely different businesses that they run.

Since 2007 I have been working as a management consultant and workshop facilitator helping clients in the software industry with global growth including building networks of independent channel partners. However, as a management consultant I can only serve a few clients at a time.

---

[17] Denmark represents less than 0.5% of the global demand for IT related products and services. Bech, Hans Peter. 2013. Entering Foreign Markets in the Software Industry - The BECH Index 2013 (TBK Publishing®: Copenhagen, Denmark).

[18] Damgaard merged with Navision in 2000 and was acquired by Microsoft in 2002.

[19] Now Microsoft Dynamics AX.

[20] HOB Business Solutions that was later acquired by Avanade.

With this book I hope I can help many more software companies around the world make the right choices on how best to serve their customers and grow their global market share, when they apply the indirect go-to-market approach.

If your choice is to build independent channel partner networks then I hope you will use this book as the "manual." As I have no interest in recommending that software executives in general take a specific go-to-market approach the book is not promoting the indirect channel approach over any other go-to-market option. This book is supposed to help software executives that - for valid reasons - have chosen the indirect channel approach and support them in getting it right.

How Many Partners do we Need?

Let me conclude this introductory chapter with a crucial question that will help clear up one of the major misconceptions of what an indirect partner channel approach is and what it is not.

How many independent channel partners do we need?

The answer to this question obviously depends on how we define our market and how much market share we are aiming for, but the indirect channel approach works best if we have a big market in terms of the number of potential customers and when that is the case then we will need many channel partners.

The answer also depends on what type of product (value proposition) we offer, and the indirect channel approach works best if our product (and value proposition) is a platform requiring channel partners to add products and services in order to deliver the whole product[21]. Then we can have many channel partners as each of them adds value

---

[21] The whole product is defined in (Moore, 2014) as the combination of products and services required to give the customer reason to buy and secure successful implementation. Happy customers serve as valuable references for further sales.

to the specific sub-segment of the market that they have decided to serve. In this scenario the channel partners do not necessarily compete for the same business and the market saturation threshold is much higher than if the channel partners are competing with the exact product for the exact same opportunities.

I often hear software executives talk about their channel partner approach only to realize that they are looking for one or two channel partners to cover a market, say, the size of Germany[22]. This book is not about recruiting one or two channel partners to cover a market the size of Germany. This book is about the situation where we need a hundred or more channel partners to secure a 20% market share in Germany and a thousand or more channel partners to secure a 20%[23] market share in North America. The numbers 100 or 1,000 are not sacrosanct. The crucial difference between the scenario with many channel partners and just a few channel partners is that in the first scenario we do not depend on the individual channel partner. Individual channel partners may come and go leaving us unaffected.

If we have the ambition of making it to global market leadership through independent channel partners, then we must accept that we need many partners and that they will often be competing for the same business. We may not deliberately include the objective of "over penetration" in our channel partner recruitment brochure, but internally we know that to make it to market leadership we will need a big channel providing a broad market reach. If five independent channel partners are competing for the same business then we prefer that they are doing it with our product rather than with the products

---

[22] Teaming up with one or two channel partners to cover a market the size of Germany is more a joint venture approach. Let's assume that the German market for our type of offering generates €1B annually. Achieving the 20% market share means managing €200M in annual revenue. With one or two channel partners taking care of such large chunks of business I can hardly imagine that we will treat them as "independent" channel partners. The more likely scenario is that we start with an exclusive arrangement and then we acquire the "channel partner" as the business becomes critical to the performance of our own company. With just one or two channel partners we have a direct Go-to-Market approach and should not mistake it for anything else.

[23] 20% market share is the tipping point after which the market dynamics change from push to pull lowering our customer acquisition cost and increasing our margins.

of our competitors. It is that simple and this is the scenario that this book is about.

This book is about building large networks of independent channel partners making us global market leaders.
Enjoy.

CHAPTER 2

BOOK SUMMARY

The software industry is full of abbreviations and labels such as ISV, SI, OEM, VAR, VAD, White Label, Distributor, Reseller etc. I have included my definitions and explanations of what they stand for in Appendix A.

The discussion of when and how to become the global market leader through networks of independent channel partners requires a conceptual framework and in chapter 3 I introduce the business model and business model environment frameworks developed by Alexander Osterwalder and Yves Pigneur. The introduction is brief and for readers who require more detail, I have an extended discussion on the frameworks in Appendix B. I conclude that our business models are completely different from the business models of our channel partners and that we need to know and master both to become successful. I also conclude that taking the indirect route to market adds a layer of complexity to our business model as we leave the control of finding, winning, making, keeping and growing happy customers to third parties.

In my humble opinion the direct and the indirect go-to-market approach are not options we can choose freely between, independent of the nature of our business model and business model environments. In chapter 4 I discuss when the indirect go-to-market approach is applicable and advantageous and when it is not, and I conclude that taking the indirect route to market requires that the channel is an integrated element of our product offering and value proposition and unfortunately not something we can easily bolt-on at a later stage.

With the decision to take the indirect route to global market leadership we need to develop and maintain a channel partner program and in chapter 5 I introduce and discuss all the elements of this program. Although we need similar types of activities when running our own marketing, sales and implementation operations, the choice of an indirect route requires more well-defined processes, more formal formats, earlier announcement of activities and events, longer lead times for changes and communication and collaboration platforms that are scalable and available 24/7. I also conclude that our partner program will change substantially as we move from early stage channel building to the mature mode where most of our revenue comes from existing channel partners.

Chapter 6 is devoted to a discussion of channel partner recruitment, where I conclude that the initial process is very similar to the process we follow when we hire top performing customer-facing staff for ourselves. The big difference is in the compensation formats; where we pay staff to perform their duties from the day they join, channel partners will have to make substantial investments before they reap the benefits of the cooperation. It is therefore more difficult to recruit channel partners than recruiting staff and it takes much longer.

Also the dynamics of channel partner recruitment changes as we move from the early mode channel development stage to the mature stage and I conclude that as soon as we have the opportunity we should recruit as many channel partners as we possibly can. We let them demonstrate where they belong in the channel pyramid that I introduce in chapter 7, where I discuss channel partner management. I classify partners as Stars (5%), Growth Potential (15%) and The Rest (80%) and discuss how we should manage each group.

As many software companies consider adopting the indirect channel approach at a later stage after having applied a direct approach first

I have devoted a full chapter to how this switch can be accomplished. I introduce some simple sanity checks to verify if switching is feasible or not and recommend an approach for making the switch successful.

Chapter 9 defines and discusses channel conflicts and what we can do to manage them.

Chapter 10 explains that distribution does not necessarily have to be performed by the software companies themselves, but in theory could be outsourced to a value added distributor and I also explain why that in practice is difficult for us in the early stages of channel development.

The changes occurring in the software industry where the cloud-based software-as-a-service format complements and often replaces the perpetual, on-premise and pre-paid license format has - and increasingly will have - a profound impact on the role and remuneration formats for independent channel partners. I discuss these trends in chapter 11 and conclude that the change in the cash-flow, the increased competition, the diminishing power of the CIO[24], the diminishing cost of application development, mobile computing and the preference for simplicity over complexity, all change the landscape for channel partners and their principals alike.

Although the formal channel partner agreement is probably the least interesting document in the context of creating a channel partner ecosystem I have nevertheless included a sample in Appendix C.

Appendix D includes a further elaboration of the channel partner P&L, which is a critical tool when recruiting and managing partners. As the channels for reaching and communicating with our customers are changing dramatically I have included a recommendation for how to include the web and social media in our channel partner management effort in Appendix E.

---

[24] Chief Information Office.

Appendix F discusses the exclusivity issue that keeps popping up all the time and everywhere. My recommendation is basically don't do it, but when we do it, then follow my other recommendations.

Finally, I have included a list of recommended literature in Appendix G.

CHAPTER 3

CONCEPTUAL FRAMEWORK

Throughout this book I will use the business model[25] framework introduced by Alexander Osterwalder and Yves Pigneur in their renowned book "Business Model Generation[26]".

> → The business model framework[27] gives us an overview, a vocabulary and a set of definitions that enable us to more clearly define, develop, understand and communicate our own business model to our stakeholders including our independent channel partners.

> → The business model framework enables us to understand and consistently discuss the business models of our independent channel partners.

> → The business model framework provides us with a structured framework for discussing and improving the impact of our partner value proposition on the business model of the individual channel partner.

---

[25] When Alexander Osterwalder & Yves Pigneur published their book "Business Model Generation" in 2010 we had already been using the term "business model" for more than two decades. The term "business model" became very popular during the first "dot com" boom at the end of the nineteen nineties. However, there was no clear and unambiguous definition or framework for explaining what a business model really is until Osterwalder & Pigneur published their book.

[26] Please see Osterwalder, Alexander, Yves Pigneur, and Tim Clark. 2010. Business model generation: a handbook for visionaries, game changers, and challengers (Wiley: Hoboken, NJ).

[27] I highly recommend that you to read the book and also to attend either Osterwalder's or my own classes on Business Model Generation. A free summary of the book is available from Osterwalder's web site. Reading the book in its' full length is highly recommendable for anyone engaged in business development, in channel development and management in particular. Visit www.tbkacademy.com for the training schedule, locations and prices.

The business model framework[28] also enables us to speak the same language as we grow the company and bring new staff members and new channel partners to the party.

THE TWO PERSPECTIVES

Osterwalder's business model framework operates with two main perspectives:

I The internal perspective: the business model (the canvas)

II The external perspective: the business model environment (the four forces)

THE INTERNAL PERSPECTIVE

The internal perspective includes those elements of our business that *we control ourselves.*

The business model is divided into nine areas or building blocks that Osterwalder has nicely organized in a graphic illustration called the *canvas* helping the people involved with defining and executing our strategy to have the exact same perception of how their business model works.

---

[28] You can find a brief summery of the business model and business model environment concepts here: Bech, Hans Peter. 2013. Business Model Generation — The Emperor's New Clothes? (TBK Publishing®: Copenhagen, Denmark).

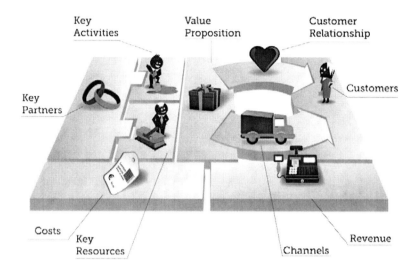

Key Activities · Value Proposition · Customer Relationship · Customers · Key Partners · Costs · Key Resources · Channels · Revenue

Figure 2: The business model canvas

THE EXTERNAL PERSPECTIVE

The external perspective includes all the elements impacting our business that we *do not control ourselves*. We call this perspective *the business model environment*. The business model environment represents the risk that we must mitigate and the opportunities that we can take advantage of and is nicely organized into four areas helping the people involved in the business development analyze, discuss and understand the external world using *the same* terminology and structure.

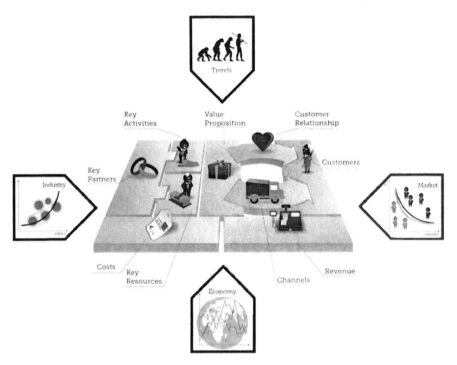

Figure 3: The business model environment

THE BUSINESS MODEL

A business model describes the rationale of how an organization creates, delivers and captures value.

We select our target customer segments, we design our value propositions to best serve these customer segments, we choose which type of relationships we will have with our customers and we choose which channels we will use to find, win, make, keep and grow our happy customers. We call this part of the business model the "**Front Office**." Our front office activities will generate customers and revenue.

In the "Back Office" of our business model we need to employ certain key resources that can execute certain key activities delivering our value propositions to our customers. The back office o ften b uilds relationships with key partners[29] and the back office generates cost.

THE CHANNEL

As you can see in the business model canvas illustration one of the nine building blocks is *the channel*.

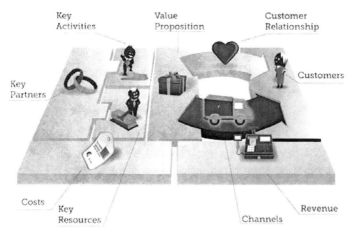

Figure 4:
The channel is one of the nine building blocks in the business model framework.

The job of the channel(s) is to find, win, make, keep and grow happy customers. In other industries the channel may have more obligations such as importing, warehousing, logistics and repair, but as the software industry operates with virtual products the channels are primarily engaged in extending the value of our products and in marketing, sales and support.

The reason that so many software companies fail to make the independent channel partner approach work can be explained using the business model framework.

---

[29] Key partners are supply chain partners that we have a strategic relationship with. These partners are different from the independent channel partners that we engage to find, win, make, keep and grow happy customers. We buy something from our key partners and we sell through channel partners. Other types of strategic alliances where there is no transactional relationship are also categorized as key partners.

Let's imagine that we have a direct channel approach and thus operate the channel with our own resources. We are in full control of all strategic decisions, of product management, development etc., and we engage our own marketing, sales and pre-sales people plus we allocate the budgets required to find, win, make, keep and grow happy customers.

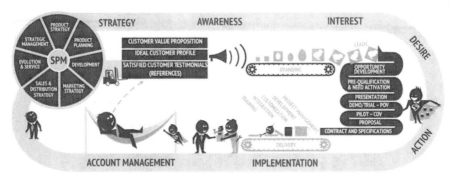

Figure 5: Typical value chain in a Level 2-3 B2B software company.
See Appendix H for an enlarged version of the illustration

Examples of the activities that we may be undertaking and constantly optimizing are illustrated in fig. 5.

Operating the activities and resources ourselves gives us overall control. We can manage all processes and resources in the constant effort of optimizing the performance of the company including our channel operations (how we find, win, make, keep and grow happy customers). It is entirely within our control to start new initiatives, monitor progress, take corrective actions and engage and dismiss resources.

When we decide to leave the responsibility for some or all of the activities concerned with finding, winning, making, keeping and growing happy customers to independent channel partners, we introduce a layer of substantial complexity.

We are introducing an independent third party business model into our own business model as illustrated in fig. 6 below.

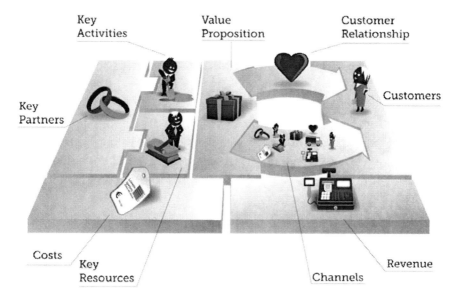

Figure 6: The indirect channel represents a third party business model in our own business model.

Independent channel partners operate their own business models and choose their own business model environments.

Building successful channel partners requires that we understand their business models[30] and manage to align them with our own business model. Our independent channel partners operate their businesses according to their own aspirations, ambitions, objectives, skills and resources. We can introduce incentives and offer support programs, but we cannot demand or control how they should run their businesses. The fundamental reason for the difference in our business models stems from the difference between our customer value

---

[30] We cannot expect that all our independent channel partners will have exactly the same business model, thus we need to understand each individual model or at least group them according to their characteristics.

proposition[31] and the value proposition of our independent channel partners. Even though we cooperate with our independent channel partners with the objective of bringing our products to well defined customer segments we do not have identical value propositions.

Software companies must be technology driven and must have product leadership as their strongest strategic value element[32]. By nature the software industry is a volume game often with network effects and "winner-take-all" characteristics. With negligible marginal production cost the economy of scale benefits are enormous and in the long run the market leaders will crush their smaller competitors. Software vendors always drive for volume through market leadership.

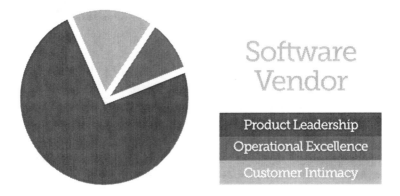

Figure 7: Software companies have product leadership as the dominant element of their customer value propositions. Operational excellence is a second priority and with the move to cloud based delivery format this component becomes more important. Only very few software companies have customer intimacy as a strong value element and if they do then they must have a direct channel approach.

---

[31] An approach to defining generic value propositions as used in this book is thoroughly described in Treacy, Michael, and Frederik D. Wiersema. 1995. The discipline of market leaders : choose your customers, narrow your focus, dominate your market (Addison-Wesley Pub. Co.: Reading, Mass.).

[32] For a definition of the value elements please see Treacy, Michael, and Frederik D. Wiersema. 1995. The discipline of market leaders : choose your customers, narrow your focus, dominate your market (Addison-Wesley Pub. Co.: Reading, Mass.)

Our independent channel partners will typically have a value proposition that is focused on the individual customer with the objective of optimizing the Customer Lifetime Value. Channel partners know that selling more to current customers is much more profitable than acquiring new customers and are therefore obsessed by maintaining and expanding their customer relationships.

They do so by sourcing products from vendors (such as us) and adding services or other value elements that match the needs of the individual customers in their target market segments. With very few exceptions independent channel partners have Customer Intimacy as their strongest value proposition element and compared to their principals they typically have relatively few customers.

Figure 8: Independent channel partners have customer intimacy as their dominant customer value proposition element. Operational excellence in project management is also important, while product leadership has insignificant importance.

The customer value proposition of a company is decisive for how to organize the rest of the business model and as the principal and her independent channel partners have completely different value propositions they also have completely different business models.

Using independent channel partners to find, win, make, keep and grow happy customers demands that we understand and manage two different sets of business models. We need to manage and optimize our own business model while understanding and motivating our independent channel partners to manage and optimize their business models so that they serve our interests. Doing so is never a walk in the park, but when it works it can accelerate our business like a booster rocket.

I will discuss later in the book that the activities and resources required for recruiting, managing and growing independent channel partners are not identical to the activities and resources required for developing competitive products that are attractive to customers and to the channel. In principle software companies may outsource all the activities associated with recruiting and running the channel to a specialized third party, but there are reasons why that works better in theory than in practice and I have a discussion of these differences between theory and practice in chapter 10.

The Alexander Osterwalder business model tool gives us the framework to understand and manage the independent channel partner approach, but the indirect channel model is always more complicated to manage than the direct model.

I have included a more detailed review of the business model and the environment in Appendix B. If you are not familiar with the business model framework in a software industry context, then I suggest you read Appendix B before you continue with the rest of the book.

Let me conclude this chapter by quoting my friend Per Steen Pedersen[33]:

If you have enough money: go direct
If you have enough time: go indirect

It is a gross simplification, because there are many more parameters to consider, but it stresses the fact that the indirect channel approach is NOT a fast route to market, but if we have the patience, then it can work wonders for us.

---

[33] Per Steen Pedersen was Executive Vice president with Damgaard from 1993-2001 and responsible for growing the global partner channel for what is now Microsoft Dynamics XAL and AX.

CHAPTER 4

WHEN TO TAKE A CHANNEL ROUTE AND WHEN NOT TO TAKE THE CHANNEL ROUTE?

Before 1990 there were not many commercial transactions taking place in the software industry without some degree of human interaction. The invention of the Mac/PC created a market for shrink-wrapped software that we could buy off the shelves in computer stores. However, getting our software to the shelves of these stores was still an expensive and cumbersome process for us software vendors. While consumers made their way to the stores to buy software, selling software to businesses was always a job involving salespeople making on-site visits, demos, proposals and so on.

The Internet has changed everything.

TOUCH LEVELS

The Internet has enabled new business models that the world hadn't seen before. The business model building blocks that have changed most are probably *The Value Propositions*, *The Channel* and *The Customer Relationships*. In this book we will talk about touch levels in the business model's *Channel* and *Customer Relationships* and I will distinguish between 3 levels of customer touch[34].

---

[34] See Figure 1 in chapter 1

Low (or no) Touch[35]

The No Touch business model is characterized by the situation where customers find us and purchase online through processes that we have defined and keep fine-tuning. No human and individual interaction with customers is required to drive and scale the business. Low Touch business models are characterized by situations where we may need human interaction in some of our customer acquisition touch-points, but we do not need an in the field operating sales force. The average sales cycles are typically very short[36] in No or Low Touch business models.

Medium Touch

In this situation we need an in the field operating sales force, but the average sales cycles are shorter than 12 months.

High Touch

In this situation we need an in the field operating sales force, and the average sales cycles are longer than 12 months.

How do these touch levels affect our choice of channel?

---

[35] Many software startups prefer the "No Touch" approach not only for scalability reasons, but also because it takes the need for a sales department out of the equation. Sales have never been a loved profession by software developers. Investors love "No Touch" based business models, as they are more likely to scale fast and efficiently.

[36] Less than three months.

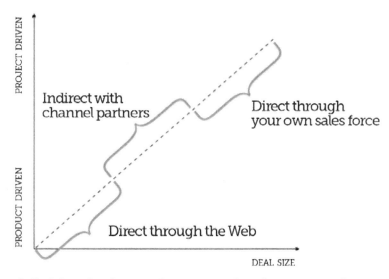

Figure 9: Guidelines for when it makes sense to take a direct go-to-market approach and for when it makes sense to take an indirect go-to-market approach.

No or Low Touch

When deal sizes are small and the functionality of the software is easy to understand then selling directly though the Internet may be the most productive scalability option available to a software company.

However, this option is only possible if there is an existing or very latent demand in the market and the potential customers can easily find us.

In order to run a No Touch business model we must be able to answer positively these five questions:

- Are there already a sufficient number of customers actively searching for solutions that our software covers?
- Can we generate enough[37] traffic to our web site where we

---

[37] Meaning that the Customer Acquisition Cost doesn't exceed the Customer Lifetime Value.

can support the customers' purchase decision?

➔ Can we provide customers with a "risk free"[38] way to try our software?

➔ Will customers make purchase decisions without any need for individual support?

➔ Can we keep and grow our customers?

The smaller and less risky the purchase decision becomes the more likely it is that we can make a "No Touch" business model work. Making software available as a service has dramatically improved the options for designing "No Touch" based business models. When we can generate "enough" traffic to our web sites, but suffer from low conversion rates then we may consider offering email, chat or other individual conversations with our potential customers. With enough inbound traffic there is room for experimentation and optimization of the conversion rates. Making "No Touch" business models work is a marketing and "growth hacking"[39] challenge and leaving this challenge to independent channel partners is guaranteed to fail.

When we have substantial inbound traffic, but still suffer from low conversion rates we may introduce an inbound telesales function reaching out to our most promising leads[40].

When we cannot drive enough organic[41] inbound traffic to our web site, when paid-for traffic is too expensive and the average customer

---

[38] Can we offer them a free trial period, a free limited edition, and/or the possibility to cancel the deal if the software doesn't meet their expectation or requirements?

[39] "Growth hacking" means finding inexpensive ways to reach potential customers and represents a race with the social, news and content media platforms that want to monetize this traffic. The hacking component is exactly searching for "free" ways to reach the potential customers.

[40] An excellent example of building and scaling inbound telesales can be found in "The sales acceleration formula: using data, technology, and inbound selling to go from $0 to $100 million" by Mark Roberge (2015) Wiley, Hoboken, New Jersey.

[41] We distinguish between organic traffic and paid-for traffic, where organic traffic comes from recommendations, referrals and postings where we do not pay a penny for a single visitor.

life-time value value can justify the effort, then our next option is typically *outbound* telesales. When we can find, win, make, keep and grow happy customers through outbound telesales we still may be able to keep costs down to avoid having to recruit and maintain an in the field sales force as we scale our market reach. If we are in a market where the average deal size is small and the sales cycle correspondingly short, direct outbound telesales may be a feasible scalability option. When our solution allows a free try/test version that only requires little customer engagement, then the outbound telesales approach can be very productive.

However, telesales is always a tough job that comes with a lot of rejection. It takes a certain personality character to thrive and succeed in this environment and the employee churn rates in outbound call centers are very high. Building and running an effective outbound telesales approach also requires highly specialized leadership and management resources.

No and Low Touch business models seldom need independent channel partners to scale. Companies with such business models are better off applying a direct approach where they can fine-tune the lead generation and conversion processes with full control over resources and activities.

MEDIUM TOUCH

As deal sizes grow so does the complexity of the customers' purchasing processes. When the price tag grows and there is also a need for specific functionality, customization and implementation services to make our product work, then intimacy and trust become important to our customers' decision-making criteria. The sales process of such Level 2-3[42] solutions requires an in the field sales capability while understanding and responding to specific

---

[42] See figure 1 in chapter 1.

customer requirements becomes vital in driving the sales processes to successful completion avoiding the expensive "silver and bronze medals[43]."

With increasing deal sizes and customized solutions come increasing margins and the opportunity of sharing this margin with independent channel partners becomes a viable opportunity. We are now moving into the zone where the conditions and opportunities for scaling our market penetration efforts favor a business model using independent channel partners with specific domain knowledge, established customer relationships, auxiliary service capabilities and in the field sales forces. This zone is also where, traditionally, channel partners are already operating and thus are available for integrating our value proposition into their portfolio. As long as there is a certain deal flow and the average sales cycles do not exceed 12 months, then a network of independent channel partners may be the best way to grow our market share and become market leaders.

HIGH TOUCH

Moving up market, where deals become even bigger, but also fewer, makes the pendulum swing back in favor of the direct channel approach. With highly complex purchase situations and only a few deals a year the independent channel partner approach is no longer a feasible option for extending our market reach. The learning curve for new partners becomes prohibitively long and spreading a few annual deals over several partners spoils the advantages of the economy of scale opportunities for all the partners.

In the High Touch zone we will meet the so-called systems integrators, who make a living off helping large customers with IT

---

[43] Any B2B sales department gets more silver and bronze medals than they get gold medals and in business only the gold medals count. If we are not careful we end up spending more time on the deals that we lose than on deals that we win. The ability to qualify therefore becomes one of the most important skills in the sales manager's toolbox.

implementation projects. If we are successful the systems integrators will be interested in the service revenue opportunities associated with our products and we may choose to work with them, expanding our delivery capacity. Unfortunately systems integrators are often prevented[44] from undertaking direct third party product sales activities and it is therefore impossible to sign them up as genuine channel partners. They are also driven by extreme customer intimacy value propositions and are therefore seldom geared for the repetitive product sales job.

Scaling our market reach through independent channel partners is a feasible necessity in the Medium Touch zone, where there is a substantial deal flow, where the average sales cycle is not longer than 12 months and where individual deals require auxiliary services giving the partner margins from other sources than just our product. The more value add the channel partners can provide the better the probabilities for making resellers successful, making them stay loyal and helping scale our market coverage.

---

[44] Many systems integrators have independency from vendor interests as a core value.

CHAPTER 5

THE CHANEL PARTNER PROGRAM

Building an indirect channel essentially requires the development of three basic frameworks:

1. An ideal partner profile
2. A channel partner agreement
3. A channel partner program

The ideal partner profile is discussed in chapter 6 while the channel partner agreement and program are discussed in this chapter.

This chapter assumes that we are in the Level 1 Early Mode[45] stage of building our channel and therefore do not operate and negotiate from a position of power vis-à-vis our potential channel partners. In this stage we need the channel partners much more than they need us. This chapter also assumes that we have a somewhat strategic and mission critical product with a medium touch[46] business model requiring an in the field sales force that can navigate the purchase process of the potential customers.

THE BUSINESS PARTNER AGREEMENT

The Channel Partner Agreement (CPA) is the legal document that we ask the channel partners to sign when we have agreed to commence

---

[45] See figure 1 in chapter 1.

[46] Level 2 customer touch and sales cycles as illustrated in figure 1 in chapter 1.

the business relationship. When we decide to change the CPA we do not want an individual discussion with our hundreds or thousands of channel partners. The CPA is therefore a document that we want to keep identical[47] for all channel partners and it is a document that we do not want to change very often. The CPA often appears as a "declaration of war" because it is written by our lawyers and first and foremost has the objective of protecting our interests and ensuring that we always comply with the local legislation. Our channel partners always have the prerogative of stopping the business with us from one day to the next, while we have an obligation to deliver and support them within a certain termination period and therefore we need to protect our rights.

We prefer to keep the CPA as short as possible and only cover those issues that are really critical for protecting our business and IPR[48], to ensure that we are law abiding and therefore we need to give the lawyers a big say. The CPA is an important, but not very interesting, document. As soon as it has been signed we don't use it unless there is a severe conflict. However, I recommend that companies in early and growth mode[49] keep the CPA simple and easy to understand. All the big software companies have CPAs that are comprehensive and complicated "declarations of war" and we might as well take advantage of our size and agility to use the CPA as a differentiation parameter proving that we are much easier to do business with.

I need to stress that doing business through independent channel partners is an area regulated by law in most countries and we therefore must comply with the local legislation. The objectives of such legislation is to ensure that channel partners are treated equally and fairly, that we comply with consumer protection and other business

---

[47] It is not possible to maintain identical paperwork across country borders as the legislation varies from country to country, but within a country we should keep the paperwork identical for all our channel partners.

[48] Intellectual Property Rights.

[49] See figure 1 in chapter 1.

regulations, that we pay our taxes and any other government fees and that our activities are not hampering free competition.

A sample Channel Partner Agreement is included in Appendix C.

THE OBJECTIVE OF THE CHANNEL PARTNER PROGRAM

The terms and conditions associated with our *channel partner* relationships are collectively known as the channel partner program. The objective of the channel partner program is to make it attractive and easy to do business with us, enabling us to recruit and manage partners to cover the full potential of our product and achieve our leading market position. The channel partner program shall support the three stages of our relationship with the channel partners:

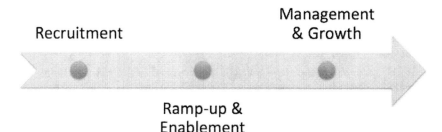

Recruitment

Management & Growth

Ramp-up & Enablement

Figure 10: The three stages of channel partner development.

    ✤   The channel partner program must motivate potential partners into talking to us and eventually signing up to include our product in their customer value proposition.

    ✤   It should motivate the channel partners to invest in the ramp-up phase, showing patience and persistence overcoming the learning curve and their initial lack of customer references.

    ✤   Finally the program should motivate the channel partners to keep growing their business providing us with increasing revenue, and thereby contribute to building a solid position vis-à-vis our competitors in the industry.

SUPPORTING THE VALUE CHAIN

Fundamentally the partner program must be designed to support precisely those activities that we ask our channel partners to assume responsibility for.

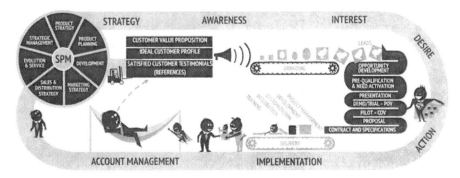

Figure 11: Examples of the steps and activities required to support a customer acquisition process that we may ask our independent channel partners to assume responsibility for. See Appendix H for an enlarged version of this illustration.

I strongly recommend that we develop our own "best practice customer acquisition process" before we design our channel partner program as each element of the program should support a step in this process. Our channel partner program is the default path from getting started to achieving return on the investment with our value proposition and running a profitable business "thereafter." It should be fair and balanced, requiring investments and focus from us and from our channel partners, otherwise it will not fly.

Our channel partner program is *not* supposed to be a free lunch where the partners can serve themselves as they please without any financial implications. However we should always - and with current technology it is also feasible to - deliver as many of the services as possible in formats associated with the lowest marginal cost[50] possible. The fundamental principle is to deliver high value that the channel partners must pay to receive and then find ways to deliver this value as inexpensively as possible. Thus our channel partner program shouldn't be a profit center, but it shouldn't be a loss center either.

The Channel Partner Program as a Recruitment Tool

In the recruitment process we will discuss how to get the business off the ground with the potential channel partners and our channel partner program should provide most of the answers to this challenge. The potential channel partners will expect us to have a plan and a program and that we are able to answer the fundamental questions related to our partner value proposition, including what it will take to win the first customers and secure a steady flow of business.

The potential channel partner may have her own ideas about what should be done, but more often than not those ideas may collide with ours. Sometimes such differences are based on genuine and factual issues, but my experience is that they are very often based on the potential channel partner's attempt to minimize her up-front investments[51], pushing the initiative, investment and risk to us. The ramp-up elements of the channel partner program must clearly spell out what each party must bring to the partnership and also how the bill is split.

The channel partner program must be documented in a presentation format that we use for discussing the business opportunity with our potential partners and in a format that we can leave behind for their review and consideration.

---

[50] An example is training, which is always a major element in our channel partner program, where we should invest in e-leaning formats, that may take some up-front investment on our behalf, but can be delivered to our channel partners at very little marginal cost.

[51] I will get back to this conflict of interest in the Channel Partner Recruitment chapter.

Many channel partners will expect us to make up-front investments in their businesses without any other commitments than "best effort" in return. We will have to manage such expectations and make them focus on the long term value of the relationship rather than the short term investments required. This is more difficult and requires more salesmanship in the early stages of channel development where we do not have any, or only very few success stories to share, but as we make partners successful the resistance will wear off and our promises for the future become more trustworthy.

STRATEGY WORKSHOP

If we are in a position where we can sign up many channel partners in a short time, then we should do so and wait and see who performs well. We can then invest our resources in the best performing partners. I will discuss this option in more detail in chapter 6.

When we do not have any, or only few channel partners and the time and effort it takes to recruit new partners is substantial, then we need them all to deliver certain levels of revenue. In this situation I recommend insisting that the partner's management team join a strategy alignment workshop defining the objectives and formulating a plan for meeting these objectives including the definition of a few KPIs[52] ensuring that we can monitor progress and swiftly take corrective actions[53].

The strategy workshop should use an insight and a management alignment tool such as ValuePartner[54] and the Alexander Osterwalder business model and value proposition canvas[54], which

---

[52] Key Performance Indicators.

[53] No plan will survive the meeting with reality and we always need to take corrective actions along the way ensuring that we deliver on the business objectives.

[54] http://valuemaker.eu/services/valuepartner/

[54] See Osterwalder, Alexander, Yves Pigneur, Gregory Bernarda, and Alan Smith. 2014. Value proposition design : how to create products and services customers want.

are simple and well-documented frameworks ensuring that we share the same terminology, speak the same language and use a common business development methodology. We should offer the format for and facilitate the workshop, including providing a successful partner benchmark scenario to which we can refer, to help our potential channel partner understand the business opportunity and corresponding requirements with our product.

Depending on the complexity of our value proposition we should allocate 1-3 days to the management workshop including an initial training session. This will provide the attendees with a brief overview of the value proposition, the ideal customer profile, the business model and the typical customer acquisition process ensuring that we all understand the terminology and methodology used. I recommend that the workshop take place close to the channel partner's premises, allowing as many of her staff members as possible to attend. The partner provides the venue for the strategy workshop and assigns key staff members to attend the workshop and we provide the format and the facilitators while a channel partner representative should document the findings and conclusions.

It is recommended that this workshop be run *before* signing the channel partner agreement. If it turns out that we cannot agree on the fundamental strategic issues then it is very unlikely that the partnership will work.

Should we charge for the workshop?

I have a fundamental principle that says that the value of anything is expressed by the price the customer is prepared to pay, meaning that when we are not prepared to pay for something then it is because it has less value for us compared to our other options. However, in the early channel development stage where we need the channel partners more than they need us, the management workshop is the investment we must make in exploring the business opportunity. The channel partner will invest her time and pay for the premises, food and accommodation and we will pay our own expenses. As the power balance shifts and potential channel partners start knocking on our door then we can reconsider the format and if we charge.

THE PARTNER P&L

The biggest challenge when recruiting independent channel partners is to ramp up her organization and get the first deals delivered to happy customers. Ramping up requires allocating people and money to the project and therefore a key result of the strategy workshop is the discussion and development of the channel partner's P&L[56] for the business with our product.

The P&L is the result of how we organize and drive the other 7 elements of the business model. We may set objectives for what the P&L should be in a certain future period, but we can only impact the P&L through the other 7 building blocks.

A normal high level P&L will look like this:

---

[56] Profit & Loss analysis

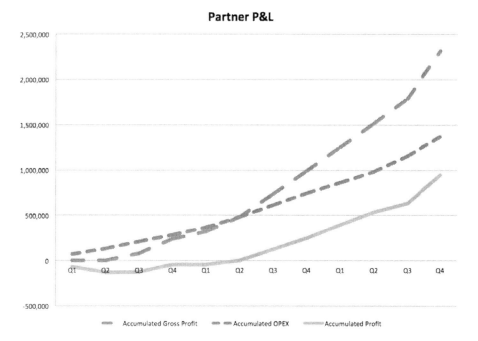

Figure 12: The Partner P&L illustrates the cost, gross profit and profit streams associated with the "partnership." All partnerships require an initial investment and have a learning curve. Rule of thumb: The larger the future rewards are the more investment and effort is required up front. Behind the P&L is a business plan spelling out what should be done when and by whom.

The issues we will discuss in the management workshop related to the P&L are:

1. What business potential do we have in a 3-5 year perspective?
2. What will we recommend that the channel partner does?
3. How will we help the channel partner to become successful?
4. What are the critical success factors?
5. What is the "time to first revenue?"
6. What is the "time to profit?"
7. How much must we invest now to bootstrap the business?
8. How much cash do these investments require?

Independent channel partners are extremely sensitive to the impact on their P&L and in general they are much more reluctant to make investments than software vendors are. Software companies are used to business models requiring upfront investment for product development with payback from license fees or subscriptions with very high margin rates. Independent channel partners are project driven service providers with people on the bench and with smaller margin rates. Making an investment in a new business ventures is much more difficult f or t he a verage i ndependent c hannel p artner than it is for the software vendor.

To help our potential channel partners review the impact of building a business with our products we must break down the P&L in more detail and make sure they are prepared to make the investments required otherwise we are all just wasting our time.

I discuss the channel partner P&L in more detail in Appendix D.

CERTIFICATION

As we start building our channel partner program and recruit the first channel partners we will typically develop our training programs first and then our certification program much later. I strongly recommend reversing the order and start with defining the certification requirements first and then developing the training program next. Having the learning objectives defined first - assuming a certain entry-level knowledge - our training program will be more logical and easier to "sell." It moves the focus away from the training itself and to the level of skills and competencies required to manage our products professionally. Our training program is one way of acquiring the skills, but the channel partners should always be free to acquire these skills through any other means.

By starting with the certification requirements first we avoid the tedious discussion with the channel partners over training. If we push training, then the channel partners will claim that they already have those skills or that we should train them free of charge.

The certification itself should be managed by an independent organization avoiding any potential suspicion that we are tweaking the requirements based on personal favors and preferences. A certificate awarded by a recognized independent organization will enjoy respect from all the players in the industry and help support our brand value.

TRAINING

Even though our independent channel partners should be free to acquire the skills required for certification where they please, we must offer a training program for all the roles required to master and build a business based on our product.

As mentioned before we need a condensed training package to be delivered as part of our channel partner management workshop. This initial training component explains the business model and how the channel partners fit into finding, winning, making, keeping and growing happy customers.

After the management workshop we must make a training program[57] available for marketing, sales and product management staff so they can launch the product and start the marketing and sales activities. Then we need a training program56 directed at the technical pre-sales people and finally a program directed at the implementation and post-sales support people.

As much of the training as possible should be delivered in an e-learning format ensuring consistent quality, accommodating

---

[57] There is no need to certify "internal" functions such as administration, marketing and product management, while it makes good sense to certify sales, implementation and support staff that has to engage directly with customers.

differences in entry level skills as well as keeping the cost of the training, including expenses associated with travel and accommodation, at a minimum. The complexity of the product and/or the operational environment may require other training formats with traditional classes and instructors.

The training should be delivered on terms and conditions encouraging third parties to enter this business and free up our resources for other purposes. As soon as we have a certain volume of such activities we may proactively engage and certify third party training companies to take over our obligations enabling us to further scale our business.

MARKETING AND SALES INCENTIVES AND REPORTING

Ensuring that the channel partners actually allocate adequate resources in getting our product in front of new customers[58] always proves to be a major challenge. Referring to the customer acquisition process described in figure 11 above we need to have programs in place to stimulate and support each of the steps.

This section on marketing and sales incentives will discuss the five main steps in the customer acquisition and management process:

1. Find
2. Win
3. Make
4. Keep
5. Grow

---

[58] Which preferably are the partner's current customers!

Figure 13: Typical sales funnel with marketing activities for creating awareness, leads and sales prospects for developing and closing qualified opportunities.

Building and managing a pipeline of business opportunities will always require a sequential series of investments and activities as signed customer contracts unfortunately do not drop out of the sky and land on our desks. Situations where we can short cut the AIDA[59] process and use existing connections to head directly for the closing phase are very rare and thus not a format that we can apply for scaling our business to market leadership.

---

[59] Awareness -> Interest -> Desire -> Action

Find

*How do customers, that need what we have to offer,
find our channel partners and us? How do our
channel partners and we find customers that need
what we have to offer?*

In the early days of market penetration where we enjoy little brand recognition in the market and have to push hard to generate a flow of opportunities we must take charge and stimulate the lead generation activities for and with our channel partners. Pushing the responsibility for building our brand and creating awareness with the first channel partners that we recruit is risky, will not scale and may provoke a request for and endless discussions about exclusivity[60].

There is no one-size-fits-all approach for building brand awareness and generating leads, but I strongly recommend having a program and a plan in place that we can adapt to the specific requirements of each country or market we enter.

I often meet software company executives that are reluctant to invest in traditional[61] marketing promotion activities and fail to understand how to engage with their target customer audience through the web and social media platforms. Most of these companies rely entirely on the hope of building a market presence through the established customer relationships of their independent channel partners. This approach should certainly be pursued as well, but if we do nothing else than I can guarantee that our business will not scale and lead to market leadership.

We will have to work to find the mix of traditional, web and social media marketing activities that engage effectively with our potential customers. A vast majority of consumers and business buyers check

---

[60] Which preferably are the partner's current customers!

[61] Advertisement, public relations, tradeshows and other mass marketing activities

their options on the Internet before reaching out to, or accepting calls from, potential suppliers. Failing to show up on the radar of our key target audiences is disastrous because it is equal to not existing. No one can do business with us if they do not know that we exist.

As this book focuses exclusively on B2B Level 2-3 business models I think it is fair to stress that the vast majority of the people in our target market segments are actually listed on the LinkedIn social media platform. By using the advanced search function on LinkedIn we can drill down to identify companies and individuals that we would like to get in touch with. Never before in the history of mankind have we had this level of transparency, yet it seems that only few software companies understand how to use this resource for engaging with their potential customers. LinkedIn is not the only place where we can engage with potential customers, but it is now the primary source of information on professional individuals including our potential partners and our potential customers.

An old saying states that *"sales is marketing, but marketing is not sales"* meaning that if I pick up the phone and call a potential customer then she will know about me and my company when the conversation ends, but seeing an ad, reading a blog post or viewing a video from my company may not make her call me initiating a sales process. That is obviously true, leading a lot of people to the conclusion that we can save the marketing budget and rely on our sales people calling potential customers.

The reason not all companies in the world rely on only having armies of sales people calling potential customers is that this approach is very, very expensive especially when we use it for early mode scaling. A mix of traditional, web and social media marketing activities and an active sales force focusing on developing the mature opportunities are required to scale our business and grow faster than our competitors.
It is beyond the scope of this book to explain how to use traditional, web and social media marketing channels to engage with our

potential customers, and if you are uncertain of how to do it I strongly recommend that you engage someone who can help you. Being ignorant of the marketing discipline is like sailing a ship without a map, compass, radio or GPS. You can sail, but it is unlikely that you will ever find your destination before you run out of fuel and food. I have included a brief and introductory discussion on the use of the web and social media in a partner channel context in Appendix E.

Win

When we have a steady flow of leads then we can start to develop them and move them through the pipeline with our partners. Although our newly recruited channel partners have certified sales and pre-sales people they still have no practical experience working with our value proposition in a real-life sales situation. To be on the safe side we should make resources available for coaching and supporting the channel partners through the first couple of deals applying the sales tools we have available.

As illustrated in figure 11 our potential customers are typically following a purchase process to assess the proposals from the various vendors and will select the one offering the best overall value proposition. Even in situations where we have activated the need and there are no competitors our potential customer will still set up a process verifying that the business case associated with acquiring our solution is competitive compared to the other investment opportunities available.

Although these purchase processes and the behavior of the various customer representatives involved are not completely identical for all projects they are certainly not completely different either. Thus we have the opportunity of developing white papers and other sales tools addressing the market challenges we know that they are facing and the concerns and the questions that the customer representatives will raise at the various stages in the purchase process. We can help our channel partners reduce the effort associated with the individual customer purchase process and thus increase their sales productivity by offering sales tools that answer typical customer questions. Applying this approach across the channel will help reduce customer acquisition costs, scale market penetration and grow market share.

Channel partners are very different and where some are self-supporting from the start, others need a helping hand. We therefore need to set a price tag on our sales support to ensure that our channel partners consider carefully whether they need us or not. The price tag can have the form of a reduced margin on our software rather than asking for cash payments, ensuring that the cash flow implication for the channel partner is as mild as possible and that we also share the risk of losing the deals.

Make

In the Level 2-3 scenario applied in this book the customer value proposition around our products usually includes a series of auxiliary services and complementary products. So that we can use the customer as a reference case and provider of testimonials we need to ensure that the channel partners can deliver the combination of products and services that meet or exceed the scope of the customer's project. Failing to do so will hurt the partner first and maybe us next.

If our products are delivered in a project context we need to ensure that the channel partners have the skills required to define, manage and deliver successfully on the scope and that the standard project management approach ties the access to our products to the channel partner's employment of certified resources. Initially this will often lead to many discussions as we are facing the chicken/egg dilemma where the channel partners may be reluctant to invest in the resources until they have firm projects and they have a hard time winning and delivering a project until they have those resources. Often the channel partners may use freelance resources that are not permanently on their own payroll and in these situations we have to be flexible until the channel has built the capacity to deliver successfully with their own resources.

If there is a shortage of certain skills in the channel then we may decide to help develop and make these resources available to the channel partners and/or customers until the channel has built the capacity. This approach may also be required when we launch new modules or products addressing segments in the markets where our current channel is not operating.

As we increase our market share we will experience situations where channel capacity becomes the main bottleneck to our growth. For products with long learning curves we may gain little by recruiting more partners as they simply "steal" the resources from our current channel partners. In this situation we need to support the influx of resources to the channel from other sources. Although many software companies would consider this a "happy trouble" situation it is not to our benefit that the channel has growth constraints and we need to actively invest in expanding channel capacity together with the channel, such as implementing recruitment and retraining programs sourcing the resources from other industries and markets.

Keep

As we grow our partner channel and provide our customers with a choice of resellers then our main objective will be in ensuring that we do not lose the customers to another software vendor. That a customer wants to be served by another channel partner is of minor concern to us other than that we need to make the transitions as smooth and easy as possible.

Our focus is less on the individual customer and much more on the market facilitating the creation of an eco-system where all our customers are offered additional opportunities and added value from third parties. If we can create an eco-system around our products we will not only give customers more options and value, but also provide our channel partners with opportunities for growing their business based on our products.

Eco-system products carry an enormous growth potential as they offer customers and channel partners more options and more value than self-contained stand-alone products.

Grow

Growing customer lifetime value is obviously closely related to what we actually have to offer the customer over the lifetime of the relationship.

We may make options and modules available that our channel partners can up and cross sell to our customers, but the optimal way to increase the CLV for our channel partners is the eco-system approach described above. We may not get a share of all the additional products and services offered around our product, but as our eco-system becomes more attractive to our potential customers and channel partners we will attract more of both and keep them longer. Eco-system products are very sticky and enjoy high customer and channel partner retention rates.

We can do much to encourage the development of auxiliary products and services by offering certification and promotion platforms and by bringing our partners and customers together to form business relationships.

SUPPORT

Technical support is helping partners to help customers use the products they have acquired and is typically organized as a separate organizational unit and cost center. Organizing and providing support is extremely important because our products often play a critical role in the customers' operation. Customer and channel partner satisfaction is closely related to the quality of our support.

We can offer technical support through various channels such as:

- A self-service web portal with access to our product documentation
- A knowledge database with answers to Frequently Asked Questions where channel partners can immediately find information on the most typical problem areas.
- A self-service web portal where the channel partners can initiate a support request
- E-mail support where channel partners can send us their questions and issues
- On-line chat
- Telephone support
- On-site support

LEVELS OF SUPPORT

Technical support is typically divided into three levels:

First line of support is the direct interface with the customers and is typically the responsibility of the channel partner. This support level should be able to solve approximately 75% of all customer support inquiries.

Second line of support takes care of issues that the first line of support is unable to handle. The software vendor organizes the second line of support, but may delegate this responsibility to a distributor. This support level should be able to solve approximately 90% of all channel partner support inquiries.

Third line of support is primarily taking care of errors or severe differences between the specifications and the documentation of the software. This level of support operates closely to the R&D function of the software vendor and only a small fraction of support issues should reach this level.

The Support System

Our support services must be managed by a dedicated support system ensuring that we keep track of the individual support case, enabling all relevant staff members access to view and update the case information and providing management with metrics for follow up, escalation and productivity improvement.

The Knowledge Base

Instead of answering the same question over and over, principals save time and money by directing their channel partners to an online knowledge base before having them submit or open a ticket or call support directly. A knowledge base can also keep channel partners updated with news, announcements, release information, and product updates.

Knowledge bases are commonly used to complement a support desk. Similar to an FAQ (frequently asked questions), a knowledge base is designed to organize and present your most common technical questions or problems and an explanation of how to solve them. A knowledge base usually stores troubleshooting information, how-to articles, user manuals, and answers to frequently asked questions. Typically, a search engine is used to locate information in the system, or users may browse through a custom classification scheme.

Product Management

The product management[62] function is responsible for maximizing the value of the product over its life-time.

---

[62] TBK Consult offers a range of ISPMA based training programs aimed specifically at the software product manager. Please visit www.tbkacademy.com for more information. ISPMA: International Software Product Management Association.

The software industry is young with companies dominated by CTOs that are also founders. Splitting their role between R&D and product management is no easy task and compared to other industries software companies have been late introducing formal product managers. Deciding to serve the market through independent channel partners accentuates the need for strengthening the product management function and introducing dedicated product managers. When moving in to new markets with new and different environments the need for formal and dedicated product managers becomes even more vital.

We are a key partner for our channel partners and they have a strong need to know what we will be offering in the future. Thus there is a need for "statements of direction," "road maps" and "release plans" allowing the channel partners to align their own business and development plans with ours.

Our channel partners will also submit an ever-increasing number of product improvement suggestions that need to be managed and prioritized. Channel partners will be frustrated if they receive no response to these suggestions, which are often initiated by market and customer opportunities that they come across.

When preparing new versions of our products the product management function assumes responsibility for the beta or field testing processes and works directly with key partners on the integration, compatibility and upgrade issues that need to be resolved before the product is released for launch.

ONGOING CHANNEL PARTNER MANAGEMENT

The partner program will define which type of business support our channel partners are entitled to. When we are in the early mode channel development stage all channel partners will receive close attention. As we learn which partners perform well and which do not we will graduate[63] the business support accordingly. I will explain how we manage the partner channel in more detail in chapter 7.

INCENTIVES

Incentives play an important role when running our business through independent channel partners. We use incentives to motivate and reward certain behaviors in our partner channel, but as the industry is constantly changing we can expect to see major alternations to the ways we encourage and motivate our channel partners.

There are three fundamental recommendations that I will make on incentives:

1. Keep it simple and don't change it too frequently. Managing incentives may consume an awful lot of resources and only simplicity and transparency can help minimize the administrative overheads.
2. We motivate and reward people, not companies. We need to understand the difference of interest between the management of the channel partner and their operational staff. Sometimes they are identical, but often they are not.
3. Our channel partners should not only make a living from the margin associated with selling our product, but from running a business around our product adding extensions and offering auxiliary services.

PRODUCT MARGIN

To attract channel partners many software companies offer higher margins than the market average. While channel partners certainly will express excitement over high margins I think it has only a limited impact on their behavior. There are so many other variables in the

---

[63] This subject is discussed further in the "Partner Management" chapter.

business model that the product margin often only plays a minor role for the channel partner, while on the other hand it often represents our only source of revenue and profit. Even small changes in the margin will have a significant impact on our profitability as we grow the channel and move towards market leadership.

My recommendation is to keep product margins as low as possible and only provide higher margins against higher levels of revenue delivered.

Helping channel partners in getting started and climbing the learning curve is much better supported with other incentives such as "free" sales and marketing support compensated by a *lower* margin on the deals.

Moving from the prepaid perpetual license model to the recurring subscription model the role of margins for our channel partners will have to be revisited and fundamentally revised. These changes are highlighted and discussed in chapter 11.

MARKETING DEVELOPMENT FUNDING (MDF)

It is normal that a certain percentage of the partner's revenue with us is reserved for future marketing actives through a Marketing Development Fund (MDF). These funds are reserved for joint marketing and promotion activities, typically on a 50/50 basis, and often on activities that we recommend. Channel partners will often try to have the MDF released for covering expenses that they have anyway and thereby making a positive contribution to their margin rather than boosting marketing and sales activities. When we are in the early channel development stage we will typically delegate MDF allocation to the partner account managers, however as we grow the channel we will have to become more programmatic and over time the MDF will typically be reserved for campaigns that we design and execute and where the channel partners can choose to participate.

SALES PERFORMANCE INCENTIVE FUND (SPIF)

SPIFs are activities and incentives directed at the channel partners' sales people. Software vendors are known for organizing SPIF days where the staff at major resellers focus on the vendor's products and are rewarded for achieving various types of sales objectives.

SPIF funds and activities are much closer to where the action is than the more marketing oriented MDF. When channel partners are carrying products that are competitive to ours, SPIF funds and activities can be an excellent way of getting more attention from sales and pre-sales people.

FUNDED HEADS

When signing on an important channel partner we may accept or even propose partial or full funding of (typically) sales resources ensuring focus and supporting the channel partner's P&L in building her business with our product.

PLATINUM, GOLD AND SILVER

Established software companies all have various levels of partnerships with their resellers leading younger software companies to believe that they need such a structure, too. In the early days of building a market position through independent channel partners we should not complicate matters with such levels. With only new and few partners they will all want to start at the top level and as we don't want a partner channel without any Gold Partners we will tend to agree. The result will be a channel of Gold Partners only, which inflates the whole concept and leaves us with the challenge of downgrading the channel partners as they fail to deliver to the thresholds.

Start with a simple channel partner structure and then differentiate later as the partners actually prove to perform very differently. We will have to redesign our channel partner structure and program as we grow our position in the market anyway and introducing channel partner classes is certainly not the first thing we should do.

BUSINESS DEVELOPMENT

Growing our business is not stimulated by monetary incentives only. Exchanging best business practices, ideas for new approaches, products and services and bringing channel partners together who can benefit from cooperating often plays a much more important role than margin, MDF and SPIF. Sharing information and reaching out doesn't come easy for most of us as we are all are busy with our own individual daily priorities. As the principal we need to orchestrate these activities, creating the platforms for the exchanges as well as crafting the content creation and encouraging sharing through the various communication channels.

With the changes currently taking place in the software industry business development and collaboration activities supporting our channel partners to build stronger business models will be much more important than the product focused margin, MDF and SPIF incentives of the past. I will discuss this in more detail in chapter 11.

THE CHANNEL PARTNER PORTAL

We cannot run a business with independent channel partners without a considerable amount of communication and reporting. We therefore need a platform for communicating and collaborating with our channel partners on a one-to-many basis, but also on a one-on-one basis concerning business performance, specific customer information, competence certificates, business opportunities and business administration in general.

Our channel partners will need 24/7 access to all the elements of our channel partner program as well as access to marketing, sales and product information. They will need access to update their own company profile information on internal and external web platforms to help them gain visibility in the markets as well as within our internal communities. They will need to place orders and access and update account and customer information and they will need access to our knowledge base and support systems for access to our roadmaps and release plans, for product specific help, for reporting bugs, inconveniences and post suggestions for improvements.

Just as our customers spend considerable amounts of time on social media so do our potential and current channel partners. I discuss the role of web and social media communication with our customers in Appendix E, but we also have a need for communicating and engaging with our potential and current channel partners through social media and to enable our channel partners to communicate with each other through social media platforms. A modern channel partner portal must leverage the power of social media and social media platforms as these have demonstrated a much better ability to engage with the audience than the more traditional "intranets."

Embarking on the indirect channel journey without a modern channel partner portal will constitute a major scalability barrier and will put a very big question mark against how serious we actually are with our channel ambitions.

Channel Partner Events

Although much can be accomplished through the channel partner portal, virtual meetings and webinars, we will still have to bring our channel partners physically together at regular intervals.

Physical events gives us the opportunity to build genuine relationships, create energy, motivate and generate the feeling of belonging to a big and warm family or an important and successful movement that is much bigger than the individual partner herself. Attending channel partner events has proven to be a very high priority with the channel partners both for business and for personal reasons.

In the early mode channel development stage where we have less than a hundred partners or so we can bring the entire partner channel together once a year in one place, but as the channel partner community grows we will need to split the events according to geography and job function.

For most software companies motivating the channel partners' executives and sales staff will initially have the highest priority and therefore the first events we organize will be aimed at this audience. However, and especially for eco-systems operators, we will soon see a need for bringing together the technical staff as well as the developers.

The importance of bringing the partners together cannot be overemphasized. To ensure that we obtain maximum impact we obviously also have an important job to do when we have all the channel partners together in one place. We need to inspire the channel partner community and recognize the most successful partners. Introducing and giving awards for outstanding and remarkable performance has a tremendous impact on channel partner motivation, one that they will subsequently use for their own promotional purposes, thus inspiring other channel partners to go the extra mile.

However, facilitating the networking opportunities for the channel partners to meet each other and form business relationships is just as important as our own inspirational obligations. Channel partner collaboration will bring additional value to our products and improve our competitive position in the market. Making other people work in our interest is one of the eight major ways[64] of building strong business models so if we have that opportunity we should certainly use it to its full potential[65].

---

[64] http://issuu.com/tbkconsult/docs/tbk-business_model_test

[65] The nature of software actually begs for designing products that have ecosystem potential. Nevertheless most software companies don't do that failing to see the opportunities or understand the requirements. If you have a software product that could benefit from being enhanced by your channel partners, then it is worth while considering how this potential could be enabled in future versions of your products and how you could help protect the investments that your channel partners are making in enhancing your value proposition.

CHAPTER 6

CHANNEL PARTNER RECRUITMENT

The process required for recruiting channel partners is very similar to the process of recruiting sales representatives for our company. First we develop a profile of what we need and then we go looking for candidates. With a long list of potential candidates we undertake interviews to shortlist the most appropriate, which we then invite to the final selection event. By the end of the process we negotiate the terms and conditions and sign the agreement[66].

The challenges associated with channel partner recruitment are also identical to the challenges associated with sales staff recruitment. Established brands get a solid stream of unsolicited applications while unknown brand names won't get any. Established brands get tons of applications when advertising, unknown brand names get very few applications, but most often they will get none at all.

If we are in the early mode channel development stage, chances are that we have no other option than getting out there and "headhunting" our new channel partners. If we have been engaged with headhunting before then we will know that the biggest challenge is not only finding the potential profiles, but also convincing them to become candidates for the position we have open. This challenge also applies to channel partner recruitment and explains why we have to go through the process of defining partner value propositions and developing partner

---

[66] If we already know a qualified candidate then we can shortcut the process and get that person on board, but we cannot rely on always knowing someone and such an approach is also not very scalable.

programs before we are ready to embark on the channel partner recruitment endeavor. So unless our potential channel partners are also actively looking for what we have to offer, then we must identify them, initiate the contact and start the process of convincing them to invest in a business relationship with us. Just as we don't want to employ sales representatives that turn out to be poor performers, we don't want channel partners that are poor performers either. As we grow our partner channel, poor performing partners will affect us less, but in the beginning we must focus and use our resources where they will produce results and simply signing numerous channel partner agreements isn't a success criteria in itself.

Defining the Ideal Partner Profile

When we recruit sales representatives for our own company we typically start with developing the job description. Based on the success criteria for the position we will first describe the job responsibilities, then we will list the professional qualifications we believe are required for performing the job and finally we will list the personal qualifications required for the job as well as those for fitting into the culture of our company. In the job advert we will also describe the opportunities and benefits we offer the chosen candidates.

In the channel partner recruitment context the job description is called *the ideal partner profile* and the opportunities and benefits we offer are called *the channel partner program*.

The ideal partner profile can be documented according the categories listed in fig. 14

The 3 sets of profile criteria

The properties of the Ideal Partner Profile are divided into 3 sets of criteria:

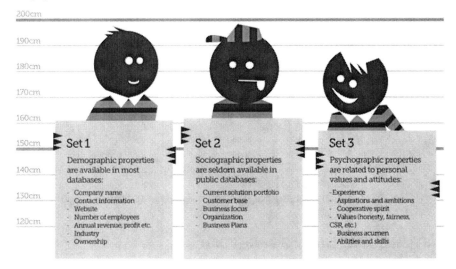

Figure 14: The three categories of characteristics used for describing our ideal partner profile.

DEMOGRAPHIC PROPERTIES

Demographic properties are company related and can easily be looked up in publicly available databases or found through simple Internet research.

Demographic properties include:

- Location
- Industry
- Financial information (revenue, profit, balance sheet, staff etc.)
- Ownership details
- Website
- Products and services offered
- Contact information

SOCIOGRAPHIC PROPERTIES

Sociographic properties are also company related and typically require interviewing key staff members and include information such as:

- Value propositions
- Current installed base of customers
- Business focus
- Organization
- Current strategy and business plans
- Characteristics of the installed customer base

PSYCHOGRAPHIC PROPERTIES

Psychographic properties are people related and require several in-depth interviews with the channel partner's management team and key team members and will provide us with information such as:

- Experience
- Business acumen
- Aspirations and ambitions
- Company culture and values
- Abilities and skills

The interviewees will not list their psychographic characteristics in bullet point format as indicated above. Someone with business executive experience must perform the interviews and the valuation of the characteristics must be based on the conversations held and the nature of the communication and correspondence through the negotiation process.

COMPETITORS AND OUTLIERS

The first issue with using the structured and logical approach for defining ideal channel partner profiles is that we often end up identifying the channel partners of our competitors. That may or may not be an issue depending on the specific situation, but we may be wasting our time feeding them information that they will channel back to our competitors and use against us in the future. We have to live with those consequences during the process of identifying those that are prepared to join us, but we need to spot those that have no genuine intention of considering the opportunity that we offer.

The second issue is that we may define a partner profile that no company will actually match, meaning that there is no existing channel that can take our value proposition to the customers. When we do not have any, or just a few partners then we need to show flexibility and accept that the channel partner that we recruit may not be a perfect match for what we would ideally prefer.

The third issue is that we will not find the outliers. Outliers are those partners that do not fit our ideal and rational profile, but nevertheless have the leadership potential to grow a business based on our products. Outliers are almost impossible to find, so we need to make ourselves visible so they can find us. When outliers reach out to us we need to apply a more flexible approach and give them the benefit of the doubt. Outliers with leadership skills can be really productive.

THE CHANNEL PARTNER RECRUITMENT PROCESS

For our core markets we will obviously have declared our ambitions and precisely stated our business objectives. Relying on random unsolicited inbound inquiries from potential partners is seldom enough to ensure that we achieve sufficient penetration capacity and market coverage, and we therefore have to identify and reach out to potential partners in exactly the same way as headhunters work handpicking the most qualified candidates.

In the early stages of building our partner channel I recommend following this process for domestic market channel partner recruitment:

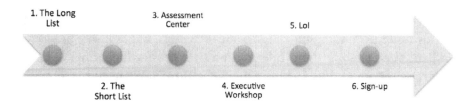

1. The Long
   List

2. The
   Short List

3. Assessment
   Center

4. Executive
   Workshop

5. Lol

6. Sign-up

Figure 15: The six steps for recruiting channel partners in markets that we are very familiar with.

As indicated above the process of recruiting channel partners is very similar to the process of headhunting sales staff. However, with channel partner recruitment there are always fewer candidates, it takes much longer than finding sales people, we are dealing with a team of people rather than single individuals, the retention[67] rate for channel partners is much higher than for our own sales staff and we are not offering any compensation package for the finalists, but rather we are asking them to make an investment against a potential return in the future. Where headhunting is something we do once in a while and where we typically engage an outside headhunter, channel partner recruitment is something we do on an ongoing basis and where we must have our own[68] resources assigned to perform the task.

---

[67] The average retention rate of sales staff is 75% meaning that we replace our entire sales staff every 4th year. Channel partners are on average with us for significantly longer.

[68] When our business model is based on building, managing and growing a channel of independent partners then doing so is a key activity, which must be performed by key resources. If we do not want to assume responsibility for the operational activities associated with the channel then we may consider teaming up with a distributor who can do this on our behalf.

Based on our ideal partner profile we can identify a long list of potential channel partners. Sources of information for the long-list are business databases, the Internet and social media[69]. The long-list should have at least ten times the number of candidates that we plan on recruiting in any given time frame in the area in question. Now we pick up the phone and call the potential channel partners on the long-list to start the qualification process. We call on the CEO[70] of the potential channel partners and if there is curiosity on her side we submit our information package. We tell her that we will be visiting in the near future and would like her feedback soon.

The steps 1-3 explained above, where the qualification process starts with the contact followed by exchange of information, should be concluded with an introductory meeting by the end of which both parties have the basis required to decide if they are prepared to take the next step. Much can be achieved through email, Skype calls and web meetings, but the final pre qualification must take place in a physical face-to-face meeting.

THE SHORT-LIST

We should expect that about half of the candidates from the long-list will qualify for the "long" short-list and we will typically have to visit all the candidates on the "long" short-list once or twice to end up with the "short" short-list.

At the personal meetings we will introduce our business proposal, including the business opportunity, present the partner program and discuss our expectations. The channel partner will present her busi-

---

[69] In particular LinkedIn

[70] Obviously depending on the size and nature of the company that we are approaching, but in most cases we deal with the top executive or at the least the person responsible for the P&L in the market or product unit where we belong.

ness and her ambitions for the future. After this meeting the potential channel partners will have to consider if this opportunity is worthwhile pursuing. Likewise we will have to consider if this channel partner has what it takes to represent our brand and perform her obligations successfully.

Our objective should be to have at least 3-4 potential channel partner candidates that are prepared to participate in an Assessment Centre[71], where we will present our partner value proposition. The potential partners will then present how they will organize their go-to-market effort and we will discuss if this business relationship can work to the mutual benefit of both parties.

The last issue to assess is the most crucial and also the most difficult: The ambitions of the management team, their motivation for investing in our product, their persistence and their ability to maneuvre and navigate through the obstacles and difficulties facing any new business endeavor. Drawing a parallel from managing staff we also know from experience that when we have to terminate someone's employment due to under-performance the reasons are 100% personal and 0% professional. The employee has exactly the same professional credentials as the day she started, but the personal qualifications were not adequate for translating the job activities into a successful performance.

It is exactly the same situation with channel partners.

We can check the potential channel partner's professional credentials, but ultimately it will be the personal qualifications of the management team that will determine performance. This phenomenon is a serious challenge when we are not well positioned in the market and the only remedy I can recommend is to recruit enough partners to make the risk of under-performance of the individual partner as small as possible.

---

[71] The Assessment Centre is typically a ½-day session where we perform an in-depth review of the potential of the business relationship with the channel partner.

We will now sign a Letter of Intent (LoI) with those potential channel partners where we see a good fit and agree on the dates for the executive workshop. After successful completion of the executive workshop we are ready to sign the channel partner agreement.

NON-CORE MARKETS

We are obviously not actively penetrating our non-core markets. Nevertheless, as these markets are typically also non-core for most other software companies we will often receive unsolicited inbound inquiries from potential partners in such markets.

Should we ignore these inquiries or deal with them?

Experience shows that most companies choose to deal with such inquiries. Experience also shows that the outcome seldom justifies the resources used. My recommendation is to set up a defense perimeter and carefully qualify inquiries from non-core markets or pass them on to some of our capable channel partners until they prove they are qualified enough for our attention.

THE CHANGING DYNAMICS OF CHANNEL PARTNER RECRUITMENT

As we move into the growth mode of the channel development stage, we can change our objectives and simplify the recruitment process considerably. We will still maintain and most likely further diversify the threshold criteria for becoming a channel partner with ourselves, but as long as newcomers meet these criteria we will sign them up without the elaborate process of interviews, assessment centers, executive workshops and LoIs. Time will then show which of the new channel partners have growth potential and we can then allocate more resources to support them. As we increase our market penetration capacity and our market share the stream of unsolicited inbound inquiries from potential channel partners will also increase and we can refocus our outbound recruitment efforts on filling out those areas in the market where we still have too little coverage.

INTERNATIONAL CHANNEL PARTNER RECRUITMENT

International channel partner recruitment typically differs from recruiting in our domestic market because of two issues:

- Different Business Model Environment
- Different Market Position

Our recruitment process therefore has an additional step.

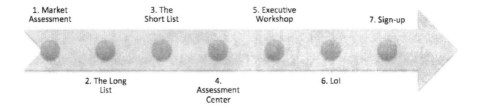

Figure 16: The seven steps for recruiting channel partners in unfamiliar markets.

We will basically always have two types of conversations with our potential channel partners:

- A product related conversation
- A commercial related conversation

Understanding the business model environment is critical for both conversations. We should never expect that the individual channel partner has a full market overview and we cannot rely on the environment perception of the individual channel partner as anything but a personal opinion. Making our own independent assessment of the business model environment will enable us to position our product in the competitive landscape and discuss the business opportunities for the channel partners based on local industry and market insight. When we move to another country we also move to another business model environment that we are much less familiar with. If we recruit partners from outside of this market[72] then we need to perform a market assessment describing the local business model environment, allowing us to position ourselves correctly and to recruit the channel partners that match our market entry strategy.

Unless we establish our own representation in the new country potential channel partners will be concerned with marketing (building awareness and lead generation) and with support. These are genuine concerns that we will have to address and the issue of exclusivity[73] will always be on the agenda as a genuine request if the channel partner is actually investing in building our brand in the market. Channel partners joining the party later will benefit from the marketing and sales activities performed by the pioneers and it is only reasonable that the latter ask to be compensated. If we are serious about building a channel then exclusivity, at least for the major markets, is out of the question and our only option is to set up local representation to take responsibility for the market building activities.

Some channel partners will also ask for the hybrid position of selling directly to customers as well as recruiting and managing resellers. This format is even more poisonous than exclusivity because the business models of a distributor and a channel partner are basically incompatible. For small and insignificant markets we may accept exclusive or hybrid solutions simply because these markets are too small to justify investing in a clean set up, but for the major markets such arrangements will always turn out to be costly in the long run

---

[72] The alternative is to establish a representation with local resources familiar with the market before commencing any recruitment activities.

[73] Exclusivity is discussed in Appendix F.

as we will need to eradicate them, clearing the way for a proper setup that can enable us to take advantage of the full potential of our products.

THE AVERAGE RECRUITMENT CYCLE

How long should we expect the outbound partner recruitment process to take?

Figure 17: In the early mode channel development stage the average recruitment effort takes much longer compared to later stages and is often a 6-9 months project.

If we are moving into a new market that we know nothing or very little about then we should allow a couple of months to perform a market assessment to help us understand if and how the business model environment is different from where we currently operate. We can also decide to gather this insight during the interviews with potential channel partners, but they may have a very biased perception of the situation and with no independent knowledge of our own we may have a difficult time filtering personal perceptions from reality. We also risk having to "pull the plug" in the middle of the recruitment process when we realize that this particular market will currently be too tough to crack with the resources we have available. Conducting the market assessment first may save us time and effort in the long run and will under all circumstances make us look much more professional when we have the first conversations with potential channel partners.

Putting together the long list of potential resellers in a new territory will take 30-60 days depending on the type of channel partners that we are looking for.

First interviews and the resulting short list should take no more than 30 days to produce. Deciding on who to bring to the assessment center and moving to the Letter of Intent stage takes anything from one to three months, and getting from the executive workshop to the signature stage normally takes 60 days.

In total we must expect that the channel partner recruitment in a new territory will take 6-9 months.

The only way we can speed up the process is by lowering the thresholds and easing the checks that we perform during the recruitment process, but the price we pay is that there is a much higher probability that most of the channel partners that we sign up will not perform. That may be acceptable if we have the capacity to sign up many channel partners, but doing so in a new territory is difficult to manage and we risk that in spreading our resources thinly they will all fail.

STRATEGIC CHANNEL PARTNER RECRUITMENT

There may be potential channel partners that will add much more than just marginal revenue to our business. Such channel partners could be recognized brands, successful with the product of our competitors, operate in a market segment where we currently do not have access or someone who would drop the product of our competitors if they switched to ours. The risk associated with signing up strategic partners is often very limited, as they have already demonstrated that they have the management skills and capacity to be successful within the domain where we operate. It makes good sense to pursue such partnerships, but we need to assign senior channel management resources to the effort. The motivation to go with us is as strategic for them as it is for us and such decisions take a long time to prepare. These decisions are finally made at the executive office, based on an assessment of the business case.

Strategic partners always know the value they represent to us and we, obviously, must be flexible if we want to bring such a potential partnership to fruition. However, until we are a major player in the market there may be situations where a potential channel partner is simply too big for us and we risk being crushed in the relationship. Big companies are political animals, with bureaucracies, shifting priorities and people moving in and out of positions. Although we may be flattered when companies much bigger than ours are interested in us and although the spreadsheet with the business case looks very promising, we should not ignore or underestimate the risk elements. They are interested in us for a reason and we must play the cards to our advantage and not be carried away by only looking at the impressive brand name and the promising potential.

CHAPTER 7

CHANNEL PARTNER MANAGEMENT

Independent channel partners do manage themselves, but not necessarily to our advantage and not necessarily with our best interests in mind. To make sure that we meet our objectives and forge the path to market leadership we must actively manage our independent channel partners.

All software reseller channels will gravitate towards the structure illustrated in fig. 18 below.

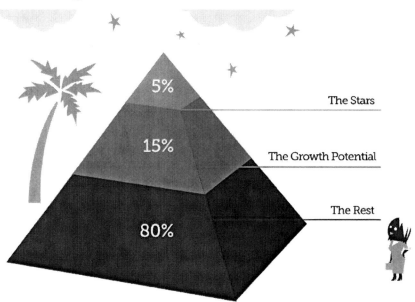

Figure 18: The typical structure of growth potential in an established partner channel, where 5% of our partners will grow by themselves, 15% will grow if helped and 80% has no growth potential whatsoever.

THE STARS

Approximately 5% of our channel partners will possess the ability to grow their businesses faster than the market without our support. The Stars set their own agenda and drive their own growth. Their leadership is ambitious, they have bold aspirations and they have the management skills required to execute their strategies. Our job is first and foremost to ensure that we are and remain an integrated part of their core value proposition and that any obstacles caused by us are removed as fast as possible. We should have no ambitions to tell such channel partners how to run their businesses, but by maintaining executive relationships we may be able to identify ways to grow together.

The management team of a Star type channel partner need and appreciate executive level input from the software vendor and do not want to "waste time" on people without decision-making powers. Our Partner Account Managers must be well connected with the top executive team of the Stars and use the liaison opportunities to build and strengthen the ties with our own executive management. The Partner Account Manager must explore all opportunities for strategic cooperation and alliances between our own company and the Stars making sure that the energy and potential of the Stars fuels the growth of our own company. There is most likely daily communication and activities between the Partner Account Manager and her Stars and there will be at least an annual strategy review and planning workshop and monthly or quarterly follow up meetings.

THE GROWTH POTENTIAL

Approximately 15% of our resellers are genuinely ambitious, but they lack the management skills required to grow beyond a certain volume of business. With external assistance they may be able to release their growth potential and become Stars. Spotting channel partners with growth potential is important, but often the signs are subtle and intangible. They are almost always great product people with weak or immature business management skills, but with a positive attitude and a curious mindset.

To release the potential we must have a general framework in place, which we can continuously improve, fine-tune and scale, allowing us to understand the shortcomings of the individual channel partner's business model and to help her grow her business around our product as the core component. In ensuring that we treat all channel partners equally, such programs must be generally available, but we can obviously define the admission criteria and the price tag to ensure that we get the right candidates into the program.

Within such a framework our Partner Account Managers become coaches and management consultants when working with the channel partner's executive level and senior sales persons when working with the channel partner's sales staff in the field. They will have weekly interactions and there will be regular strategy reviews and planning sessions plus monthly follow up meetings.

Frameworks for releasing growth potential are expensive; each program must run for several years and they will have limited impact unless the channel partners are highly motivated to join, comply with our requirements and invest in the effort. No business development program can guarantee success by laying out a predefined path and although the framework may have our support the outcome is exclusively the responsibility of the individual channel partner. To avoid any responsibility for the final outcome of such frameworks and to avoid building our own staff of "management consultants" we may assign such business development frameworks to third party service providers, where we help design and fund the program, but where the channel partners contract directly with the third party.

THE REST

The remaining 80% of our channel partners are either without ambitions or their management skill sets are so weak that no external support will have any impact on their growth capabilities. As all channel partners start small[74] we need to keep an eye on their progress to decide when to reclassify them and increase the investment in their development.

We cannot waste Partner Account Manager resources in managing channel partners who do not have any growth potential! The cost/benefit ratio will not justify the effort and the opportunity cost will be overwhelming.

Although the majority of channel partners do not have any growth potential, they still represent an important source of revenue, are a market coverage resource and often serve as subcontractors to the more successful channel partners. They should primarily be managed through the partner portal with opportunities for chat, call centre and email communication.

THE PARTNER RELATIONSHIP MANAGEMENT SYSTEM

Making it to market leadership through independent channel partners requires a Partner Relationship Management system (PRM). Just as most companies have CRM processes and systems to manage their customer relationships, an equivalent approach is required for managing channel partner relationships.

The PRM supports the channel partner relationship management processes, thus we must define these first and then implement the system afterwards. There is no way we can enforce "best-practice"

---

[74] Even large companies that we recruit will start with no revenue and just a few people assigned to our product line. The business unit is a small company in the big company receiving little top management attention until they show impressive numbers.

approaches and share crucial information about our channel partners, their performance and their issues if all the data is only in the hands of our staff who may come and go. Enforcing the systematic use of a PRM system is a genuine leadership task in our own company. Motivating our channel partners to use the system is obviously an even bigger leadership task and the secret lies in simplicity, need and value.

Making something easy and simple to use is actually very difficult, so we probably need to find software and assistance from companies that specialize in building such PRM systems. If it is easy for the independent channel partners to find what they are looking for by using the PRM system then they have less need for calling the Partner Account Manager or for giving up and failing. Managing the incentives, including the leads that we allocate, the specials bids we approve, the MDF we make available and the events we organize should obviously only take place through the PRM, ensuring that our channel partners become familiar with using the platform.

PARTNER ACCOUNT MANAGERS

The stages of starting, growing and managing a partner channel require completely different skill sets.

STARTING a channel requires salesmanship, entrepreneurship and business acumen. Our channel recruiters and partner account managers must think on their feet and re-invent the Partner Program as they move along. They must be in the front line with the channel partners, developing the business and closing the deals. We need cowboys to start an indirect channel. It may not look pretty, but the jobs get done.

GROWING a channel requires lieutenants. We cannot change the Partner Program and the Channel Partner Agreement for each new partner and we increasingly need to treat channel partners equally.

We need people who can manoeuver within the framework and not constantly change the framework. However, as we are still in business development mode, we need commissioned "officers" t o l ead t he endeavors and report back on issues that have global implications and that we must consider correcting in the continuous effort of improving our partner value proposition.

Moving into **MANAGEMENT** mode where the bulk of our business comes from existing partners we need a "Channel Partner Management Factory" for all the small partners with little growth potential, while we need business consultants for the Growth Potential and executive cowboys for the Stars. We need senior business developers for Channel Partner Recruitment, focusing on strategic relationships while mass recruitment is now in the hands of marketeers with rich self-service web portals.

CHAPTER 8

SWITCHING FROM DIRECT TO INDIRECT

Many software companies that start with serving their domestic market directly consider switching to an indirect approach only when they need to set up regional satellite offices o r m ove i nto f oreign countries. The motivation for these considerations is typically the size of the investments required for setting up and managing remote operations and the complexity associated with operating in markets where we have little or no experience.

While setting up and managing remote operations is a very difficult and risky affair it is unlikely that the change of channel approach is the right solution to this challenge. There must be very good reasons for why we have chosen a direct approach in the first place and there must be very good reasons for why we haven't made the switch in our domestic market before we apply it somewhere else where our market insight, brand recognition and management capacity is much weaker. However, let's assume that the switch is justified and that there is also an opportunity for making the switch in our domestic market; what are the steps we need to take to make it happen?

The first challenge is that we have no experience with taking our products through a channel and we therefore have very little experience with what the business model of our channel partners will actually look like. The second challenge is that we do not have the organizational set up for recruiting and supporting an indirect channel and the third challenge is that our value proposition is geared towards serving customers directly and we do not have a proven and verified role for the channel partners.

My recommendation is to therefore make the transition in two steps.

STEP ONE - SPLITTING OUR COMPANY IN TWO

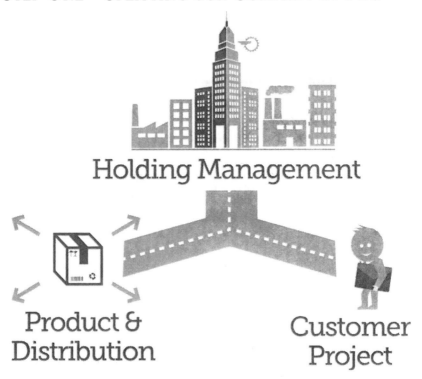

Figure 19: Switching from a direct to an indirect go-to-market approach will require that we split our company into two separate business units.

We separate the customer facing activities from the product development and distribution[75] activities. In this way all our own customer-facing activities become our first "channel partner." The two business units should not have the same management and they should operate at arms length. In this way the Product & Distribution business unit is forced to develop the value propositions, the skills

---

[75] I call this function "distribution" although we are not talking about a logistic operation. The role of distribution is to build the brand in the market and in recruiting and managing channel partners.

and the competencies required for serving channel partners and they are forced to live on a P&L that doesn't require project revenue. If this is possible then we should even take it so far as to make a divestment capitalizing the value of our customer facing activities and help in sponsoring the expansion of our product and distribution activities. A divestment will also help convince new potential channel partners that they will not experience channel conflicts[76] with us.

If it turns out to be close to impossible to split the company then chances are that we do not have a business model that is currently appropriate for an indirect channel approach. If we need project revenue to sponsor our product development activities then we are either still in start-up mode or we are not really a product company, but rather a service company with a product. If we are a service company with a product, then we may be better off carrying on like this or migrating to someone else's product platform in the future.

When we are considering making the switch from direct to indirect then I recommend making the above exercise in a spreadsheet first and if we cannot split the organization and make both business units profitable "on paper", then we have a genuine problem that needs fixing first.

STEP TWO - BUILDING THE "DISTRIBUTION" MUSCLE

If the split is possible then we can free the resources required for channel recruitment and management. We may also have to reorganize our R&D, support, product management and product marketing functions to support a channel partner approach. Whether there is a need for recruiting more channel partners in our domestic market obviously depends on the market share we enjoy. A market share of less than 20% will normally call for more channel partners,

---

[76] Channel partners are extremely sensitive to channel conflicts and a joint ownership situation will damage our recruitment efforts.

but it really depends on the size of the market, the competitive situation, and the number of deals active at any time as well as the opportunities for additional market segmentation.

The split will actually be most demanding for the customer facing organization that now has to change the value proposition from being product focused to becoming much more customer intimacy focused. The customer facing organization must have the freedom to kick out our product if this is a better business decision than staying with us. It must be up to us to make our channel partner value proposition more attractive than that of our competitors otherwise we stand no chance of winning new channel partners anyway, not to speak of replacing the products of our competitors.

CHAPTER 9

CHANNEL CONFLICTS

We define channel conflicts as the situation where our *channels* compete with each other for the same business.

FROM DIRECT TO INDIRECT

Channel conflicts often happen when we run a direct channel approach and want to reach new market segments through independent channel partners. These typical situations are when we have a strong direct position in the enterprise segment, but believe that there is an opportunity for our products in the mid-market also. As the mid-market is huge with very diverse needs, and as our brand may appear somewhat daunting for a mid-market customer then it seems obvious to take the indirect route especially if there is already an established network of independent channel partners serving the customers with similar or complementary products. To manage this situation we will normally introduce a market segmentation definition that clearly spells out where we operate directly and where we will not be in direct competition with our independent channel partners.

As the resources and activities required for recruiting and managing independent channel partners are different from those required for serving the customers directly, we would need to have separate teams assigned to each channel. Although we have defined the segmentation very clearly we cannot prevent inbound opportunities from crossing our channels and very soon we will have our own direct sales staff complaining that channel partners are fishing in our own segments and channel partners will have similar complaints with traffic in the other direction. Even in situations where we use different channels for different products there will be friction between the two channels. The situation described above applies to many of the big brands in the software industry and is something they have to manage on an ongoing basis. Smaller software companies with small market shares should avoid channel conflicts, as they can be very costly, absorbing management attention and prejudicing the motivation for new channel partners to sign up.

FROM INDIRECT TO DIRECT

The exact opposite, where we serve a market through independent channel partners, but where new opportunities demand a direct approach, is also possible. We may have opportunities in market segments where our current channels have no reach and where we fear that building an indirect channel first will take too long. In this situation we may choose to make a direct move to secure fast penetration and a position in the market and then later, if and when the channel matures, we may spin off the activity and return to our indirect channel approach.

WHITE LABEL AND "OEM" CHANNELS

A white label customer[77] renames and re-labels our product and takes it to markets where it pleases her, mainly in direct competition with our independent channel partners. An OEM customer uses our products as an integrated part of a bigger solution that she also markets where it pleases her, and potentially in direct competition with our independent channel partners. As white label and OEM customers typically enjoy much higher margins[78], they potentially

---

[77] White label and OEM businesses are our customers not our channels. As their customers have no affinity for our brand and should not even know that we exist we cannot consider them our customers.

[78] The higher margins reflect committed revenue

have a strong position vis-à-vis our independent channel partners. It is very difficult t o k eep t he l id o n w hite l abel a nd O EM d eals in the software industry and such arrangements will inevitably lead to channel conflicts with our independent channel partners, who are promoting our brand. That may or may not be a serious issue depending on our position in the market, but it will consume internal resources managing the complaints and grievances from our channel partners. However, do we truly win additional market by accepting white label and OEM deals or could we cover these market segments by actively working with independent channel partners and benefit from the additional brand recognition and awareness? I recommend that we carefully consider the long-term value of white labels and OEM customers if we also want to build and motivate independent channel partners operating with our own brand. I think that in most cases we will find that white label and OEM customers do not work well alongside independent channel partners.

OVER-PENETRATION IS NOT A CHANNEL CONFLICT

Please note that we do not consider the situation where the channel partners in *the same* channel are competing with each other as a channel conflict. Although our channel partners may complain about over-penetration they often tend to forget the benefits we all enjoy from the market leadership position when customers ask for proposals from channel partners carrying the same product. Business and government procurement policies often dictate a rather strict "request for proposal" procedure asking several vendors to submit quotations and it is one of the major benefits of operating a partner channel that customers have a choice of suppliers for the same product.

Over-penetration occurs much earlier if there is no value-add opportunity associated with our products. Products with no value-add are seldom good candidates for the independent channel partner approach in the first place. The situation is also much more fragile for us as the switching cost for low value-add products are correspondingly low. It is therefore very difficult to secure adequate penetration when taking a low value-add product through independent channel partners.

As the value-add component of a solution based on our product increases, the risk of over-penetration diminishes as the independent channel partners have opportunities for specialization and differentiation. As we develop the channel we will work with the individual channel partner encouraging and supporting her specialization into horizontal and vertical market segments and promoting cooperation wherever possible. Although we cannot (and should not) avoid a certain degree of competition in the channel we are much more concerned with having our channel partners competing with our competitors than with each other, and we should put programs in place to support this.

CHAPTER 10

DISTRIBUTION

The activities associated with recruiting and managing independent channel partners are often called "distribution." In the past most software companies with Level 1 value-add products outsourced these activities to independent distributors. For Level 2 type software companies, the traditional distributors were never an attractive growth solution and even though some software companies started out this way, most have ended up taking care of distribution themselves.

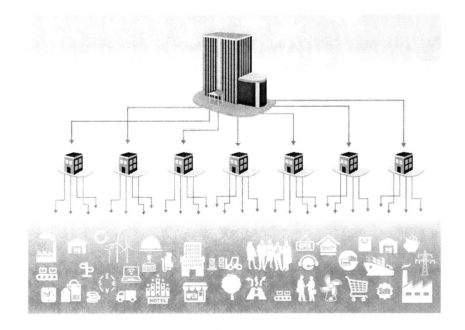

Figure 20: Distribution is a separate discipline that is not necessarily closely related to R&D

As mentioned in the introduction, distribution excellence requires different management skills, activities and resources than product excellence and theoretically it shouldn't be impossible to operate these two disciplines in different profit centres and in different legal entities. The reason that distribution remains an in-house core competence for most Level 2 type software companies is that leaving it to a third party often becomes an intolerable risk on the journey to market leadership. This, however, may change in the future.

At the Level 3 channel development stage, we are starting to enjoy market recognition and have a huge channel with a score of top performing partners. We have a small group of partners with growth potential and a large group with no major growth potential. At this point in our development, the independent distributor option seems to kick in. Over the last 10 years we have seen a revival of the so-called value added distributor whose core competence is not logistics but rather channel recruitment and management.

TIERS IN THE CHANNEL STRUCTURE

Many young[79] software companies considering the indirect channel approach initially have a simple 1-tier structure in mind:

Vendor › Channel Partners (› customers)

Starting from scratch we will typically pursue the simple 1-tier set up first. As our reach and the numbers of partners grow we will benefit from being closer to the best performing channel partners. We will have partner account managers located remotely minimizing travel cost/time and we also need remote staff dedicated to recruiting more (and more strategic) partners. If we look at the successful[80]

---

[79] Level 1 Company Maturity

[80] Level 2-3 Company Maturity

software companies with an indirect channel based approach they mostly have this intermediate structure:

Vendor HQ › Vendor Country/State Subsidiaries › Channel Partners (› customers)

Growing the channel to market leadership requires that we have resources on the ground in our core markets. As the number of people in our company grows, and in order to comply with local legal requirements, we will have to establish legal entities in the various markets.

The really successful software companies have this mature structure:

Vendor HQ › Vendor Regional HQs › Vendor Country/ State Subsidiaries/Distributors › Channel Partners (› customers)

Which structure is required obviously depends on the size of our market and which growth investments we can "afford" at any given level of our company maturity. However, if we have a solution that addresses a large market then it is unrealistic to expect that we can achieve global market leadership with a simple 1-tier[81] structure with a single operation in our domestic market and non-exclusive independent channel partners all over the world. Although most small Level 1 software companies can hardly imagine a global operation with regional headquarters and country subsidiaries, that is where the journey will lead us, however, if we have ambitions of global market leadership.

---

[81] On the other hand, if we have a very specialized solution addressing just a small niche market then the type of channel approach that this book is about, may not be applicable at all.

INTERNATIONAL DISTRIBUTION

As we move into foreign markets numerous issues[82] speak in favor of engaging local partner recruitment managers and subsequently partner account managers. We may place a lucky punch and recruit the first 1-2 innovative partners remotely, but growing beyond that will require some level of dedicated in-market resources.

As there are certain critical activities that non-exclusive independent channel partners are notoriously disqualified to perform and also have little incentive in doing, we will have to execute these activities ourselves in each of the markets/countries where we choose to operate.

Such activities are:

→ Market assessments, competitive positioning and the choice of penetration strategies

→ Product management and localization

→ Product marketing, branding and awareness building

→ Lead generation

→ Participation in major national and international exhibitions and conferences

→ Data centre operations (if we provide a cloud based format and store customer sensitive data)

Building market leadership without anyone to take care of these activities will be close to impossible and as the business model environment is different from region to region and country to country, we need to employ the resources to undertake these activities. There is a widespread perception in the software industry that

---

[82] The business model environment is different from country to country. We need market insight and local resources that know how to operate in the local environment and that may already have an established network that we can take advantage of.

working with independent channel partners negates the need for regional organizations and country subsidiaries. That is not the case. When preparing for the path to global market leadership through independent channel partners we must consider what the blueprint for the final setup will look like and then reverse engineer the process to ensure we get to where we want to be.

The main challenge we face when growing beyond our local borders is the difficulty i n r ecruiting a nd m anaging p artners w ithout a ny local presence in the new markets. Setting up this presence requires investments abroad, but also a strengthening of our own leadership and management infrastructure at home to deal with our new and growing remote operations. As our growth ambitions and the small window of opportunity push us to move into several markets simultaneously, we may not have the resources available to do so. The risk and uncertainty may be of a magnitude that endangers the life of our company. Thus sharing the investment and risk with someone who is better positioned in the individual markets makes a lot of sense, and there may actually be ways to do so.

Leaving the task of building a market from scratch to a traditional distributor on traditional terms and conditions is doomed to failure. It is unlikely that any third party will be prepared to make the investments required to build a market only to get a share of the future revenue. However, if we are prepared to share the value we create and the distributor is prepared to allocate dedicated resources to a separate business unit, and preferably operate this unit in our name, then we can define a pull-clause where we can take over the operation at a later stage. In this scenario we are actually forming a joint venture with the distributor and we are sharing the rewards of the results in terms of profits and equity, too. Such distribution joint ventures must be bilaterally exclusive and can help us accelerate the penetration of large domestic markets as well as foreign markets.

The challenge is to find individuals or companies that are prepared and bolstered to form joint ventures and that are also capable of actually building the market. Finding the right joint venture partners can work wonders, but teaming up with the wrong partners will slow us down and may damage our position and reputation within a market. Although this approach has been taken successfully in the software industry, the circumstances have always been very situational. Convincing the first one or two joint venture partners to invest in our project will be very difficult when we only have Excel spreadsheets and do not have any real-life examples to support our business case.

SUBSIDIARIES

If we cannot find an adequate distributor or a joint venture partner or if we prefer full control from day-one then we will set up a fully owned subsidiary to run the activities required to build the market. This is the traditional approach of US software companies building global market leadership. Having a domestic market that represents about 40% of the global demand will allow Level 1 US-based software companies to grow large enough to afford the management resources and command the funds necessary to take this route.

Level 1 software companies originating from smaller markets seldom have the funds or the management resources to take this route and will typically be looking for value added distributors or joint ventures. However, the supply of value added distributors or joint venture partners are extremely limited compared to the supply of employees prepared to work for us on an attractive compensation package. As mentioned above value added distributors or joint venture partners will prefer the more established brands with proven track records.

Hiring our own staff may be the only option available to us if we want to conquer foreign markets, but even then there are more challenges to overcome. Finding staff that can build a business from scratch are a more scarce resource than those who can manage an established business. Level 2 type software companies with an entrepreneurial mind-set often overestimate their attractiveness vis-à-vis the labor market in the markets they are about to enter. We always face stiff competition from our Level 2-3 domestic incumbents as well as from the bigger international insurgents. Appearing attractive to the pool of top performing professionals that can build the business for us requires a package with a superior customer value proposition for a well-defined market segment, a very proactive and attractive partner value proposition, and an attractive compensation package for the individual showing that we also believe in the venture. Candidates will judge us on our web presence, the quality of our materials and the behavior we demonstrate throughout the search and selection process. We obviously need to be equally critical because picking the wrong people will cost us dearly in lost market opportunities and leave us at a disadvantage in the race for market leadership.

VALUE ADDED DISTRIBUTORS

Just as many thought that the distributor in her role as "the middle woman" was a dying breed, we see a revival of the value added distributors. We have already discussed and concluded that distribution and product development doesn't have to reside under the same roof, but why do we see this revival just now?

Software companies in stage 1 and stage 2 channel development will have difficulties a ccepting t he r isk o f o utsourcing d istribution and they will also have a difficult t ime m otivating v alue a dded distributors investing in channel development when their brands are yet unrecognized and market pull is non-existent. However, stage 3 software companies with a large and mature installed base of channel partners may be motivated to take this path. The risk to the value added distributor is lower and therefore more acceptable.

Value added distribution excellence is 25% product knowledge and 75% business development and management knowledge. A dedicated and focused organization is actually much more likely to become an expert in this discipline than an organization mainly focused on product excellence.

All distributors have been squeezed in their traditional logistic domains. Some of them have developed their value added competences, creating auxiliary revenue streams and defending their margins vis-à-vis the vendors, and they are now available to serve more software companies. The software companies on the other hand are also squeezed by steadily increasing competitive pressure and by the shifts from the up-front perpetual license model to the subscription based cloud delivery formats. To compensate they have to shift the investments in channel partner recruitment and the cost of channel partner management to the partners themselves. With channel partner activities being only 25% product related, a model where all the cost of channel partner development and management has to be covered by the product margin is simply not sustainable.

If the value added distributors manage to provide their channel management services in a cost effective format I see opportunities for a growth scenario in the sense that software companies will be prepared to outsource these activities. The channel partners need to accept that they increasingly have to pay for the support they receive and when they do so then the business case for growing an industry of independent value added distributors might show black figures on the bottom line.

CHAPTER 11

SOFTWARE AS A SERVICE

Cloud-based SaaS is a delivery format. However, due to other changes in the market dynamics this format will gradually reformat[83] the landscape for Level 2-3 type vendors and their independent channel partners.

SOFTWARE SHOULD BE FREE OF CHARGE

That software should be free of charge is not an opinion, but a consequence of market dynamics. In any market with perfect competition the price of any commodity will gravitate towards the marginal production cost. What is the marginal cost of producing an additional copy of a software product or adding an extra user? It is very close to zero. This is exactly the principle supporting business models where the software is provided free of charge, but where the services or some extensions around the products come at a cost.

The reasons that software companies can get away with charging for their products are differentiation in functionality, managing competitive positioning and the creation of customer preferences. All of us want to be on the demand side of markets with perfect competition, but none of us wants to be on the supply side and we therefore constantly differentiate through segmentation, additional product functionality and marketing communication. So far that has worked well in the software industry, but the dynamics in our industry are changing rapidly and our customers have also learned a lesson or two.

---

[83] For a thorough discussion of this challenge see: Wood, J. B., Todd Hewlin, and Thomas E. Lah. 2011. Consumption economics : the new rules of tech (Point B Inc.:California).

SIMPLICITY DEFEATS COMPLEXITY

SaaS offerings have started with easy to understand and inexpensive standard applications for the volume markets. The enterprise and SMB markets have been apprehensive in embracing the new format due to security, privacy, survivability, availability, performance, customization, integration, payment and SLA[84] issues. However, as the compelling benefits of using the SaaS format also apply to the enterprise and SMB markets and as the issues mentioned are being addressed, we will also see deep penetration of the off-premise service-formats into these market segments. The adoption has already started with non-mission critical standard applications and will gradually move into the mission critical areas. I expect that the diminishing cost of application development and the readiness of the enterprise and SMB markets accepting best practice business procedures in non-competitive areas will pave the way for more out-of-the-cloud standard application functionality.

The rich functionality race is (almost) over and customers increasingly prefer simple solutions with short learning curves, little lock-in and no up-front investments. The CIO residing over the organization's IT resources cannot maintain her gate keeping role as software becomes available with no need for IT infrastructure, no need for platform compliance, no (desperate) need for integration and no need for CapEx[85] decisions. As software penetrates all corners of the organization and becomes available as described above, the users themselves will start to make what were previously IT-department purchase decisions.

It is unrealistic to expect that the Level 2-3 type vendors will be able to serve all these customer segments directly. The need for independent channel partners developing vertical and horizontal functionality as

---

[84] Service Level Agreements

[85] Capital Expenditure

well as providing services will therefore continue and even increase, although their roles and remuneration formats will change. SaaS will lower the thresholds for penetrating new application areas and channel partners must size up these opportunities and provide their software extensions and consulting services using the platforms of their principals.

There will continue to be a need for bespoke development, customization, integration and implementation services, but this is not where the growth will be. I expect that the need and demand for business process optimization services will grow steadily as enterprises and especially SMB customers continue to invest in using IT-technology to improve the productivity of their operations as well as to improve their customer relationships. But I expect that B2B customers will increasingly understand that there is a huge productivity opportunity in using business consultants with application software insight that can help adapt the business processes to the software rather than the very expensive other way around. Independent channel partners with staff who have both industry domain knowledge and application insight will be in high demand, and this is where the partners need to go.

MOBILE

The iPhone changed the mobile phone market and as the competitors follow suit the change is taking on tsunami-like dimensions. Mobile is in itself a cry for simplicity and specialization that opens new market opportunities every day and sizing up these opportunities will also take the cooperation between the Level 2-3 software companies and their independent channel partners. It makes no sense that each app and html5 solution provider should develop the entire stack from scratch, thus the principal/partner relationship represents the fastest and most cost-effective go-to-market approach for everybody. Today too many independent channel partners leave the mobile application market to specialized insurgents, missing the opportunity of leveraging their industry insight to embrace this business and revenue opportunity. The principals as well as the independent channel partners have to get their act together if they want to tap into the growth of the mobile application market and prevent the insurgents climbing up the anchor rope and taking the entire ship.

Pay As We Go Gives Full Insight

Moving IT out of the CapEx budget is a godsend for the majority of business customers all over the world, even when accumulated payments may exceed the alternative up-front loaded model. Combined with the option of canceling subscriptions at will the risk of IT-consumption is moving from our customers to us vendors. This is good news for all the reasons that I mentioned above and bad news if the customers churn too fast. However, as we provide our software solutions in a service based format we get something in return that the on-premise didn't provide: insight. We can actually see how users are using our services and where they have issues and challenges and with this insight we can do something about improving the value and minimizing the churn.

This is a new discipline for both the software vendors and their independent channel partners, but not for their competitive SaaS insurgents. As the independent channel partners will continue to face the customers they now need to learn data analytics and react to the KPIs on a regular basis and we as software vendors will have to provide the tool-sets for reporting on how the customers are actually using the software and other IT resources.

Cashflow

The most obvious difference between the perpetual paid up license model and the SaaS format is the cash flow profile. Instead of paying the full price up front and maybe an annual maintenance fee the software industry has settled on offering SaaS via recurring subscriptions. When these subscriptions are cancelable on short notice we introduce a risk element that may or may not have an impact on the predictability of the cash flow depending on the stickiness of our products. Solutions from Level 2-3 value-add vendors are very sticky and customers will not jump ship easily and without a long migration period. The new cash flow profile is definitely a short-term headache for everyone involved even though I believe that the accumulated Average Customer Life Time Value will actually increase.

I am prepared to take a bet on the stagnation of the on-premise CapEx-based IT format, but just as the mainframe didn't die overnight, CapEx based IT formats will prevail, but the growth will be elsewhere. The benefits of simplicity and of moving IT expenses to the OpEx[86] area are so huge that companies will not want to move back and new customers will jump directly to the new formats. We will all have to learn how to run our business models in a pay-as-you-go OpEx mode where cash flow is much closer to the customer's actual and successful consumption of our services.

CUSTOMIZATION AND INTEGRATION

Until now, cloud-based software solutions have been less open for customization and integration with other applications leaving independent channel partners with fewer options for direct application related services. This is changing rapidly as SaaS vendors discover the eco-system opportunities of having independent channel partners that offer additional functionality and services, extending the reach of their platforms and making their value proposition more comprehensive and attractive.

We have seen and I believe we will see many more examples of Platform-as-a-Service offerings where independent channel partners will use the platform's basic functionality and build their own vertical

---

[86] OpEx: Operating expenses that we pay closer to the consumption of the services.

and horizontal applications within or outside the platform through open and well-defined web services. The value of eco-system based business models is widely recognized and I see no reason why SaaS providers should not want to drive in this direction in spite of the short term-profit opportunities of serving customers directly.

Margins and Customer Relationships

Compared to the perpetual paid up license format SaaS vendors offer lower margins, not only due to the inclusion of the IT-infrastructure and the SLA obligations, but also because the competitive pressure builds up. As the cloud based SaaS business matures I expect that the traditional margins as we know them today will disappear completely and be replaced by a finders fee leaving the independent channel partners relying entirely on the value of their own extensions and auxiliary services essentially becoming mini-ISVs, implementation partners, system integrators and business consultants. The customer relationship that in the on-premise format resided with the independent channel partner will be divided between the SaaS provider for the core platform services and the channel partner for her added value. However, I also foresee that the SaaS providers will implement market places making it easier for the channel partners to promote their extensions and services, increasing the volume opportunity and lowering the CAC.

Incumbents and Insurgents

All the big Level 2-3 software brands understand that the route to maintaining long-term competitiveness and growth is not navigated by cutting off their partner channels and serving their customers directly. However, the competitive pressure is high and insurgents are inventing new business models driven by lean organizations and without any legacy formats to pay attention to. The Level 2-3 software brands will push their channel partners to rely more on extensions and the auxiliary services and less on the margins from the subscriptions and those partners that manage the change will be able to take advantage of new types of benefits offered by the vendors. The specialized insurgents will overpower those channel partners that learn too slowly. That is not only a problem for the partner, but also for the principal that now loses a player covering a market position. The principals as well as the independent channel partner has a strong common interest in figuring out how to operate in the new business model environment or they will all suffer.

SaaS and the cloud is not the end of the world for the independent channel partner, but it is certainly a dramatic change in the business model environment that offers opportunities as well as threats. The software industry is fairly young and has been faced with continuous disruption along the road. The Cloud, SaaS and mobile delivery formats represent such disruptions that will stimulate further market growth, but which will also require changes on the supply side of industry. Those that adapt may survive and grow and those that resist and despair will fail and vanish.

APPENDICES

APPENDIX A

Through my many years working with building networks of independent channel partners and consulting on the subject I have come across many entertaining and interesting definitions in the software industry. To avoid any confusion and misunderstanding I will give you my definitions of the software industry jargon related to the channel. You may not agree with my definitions, but at least you will know what I am talking about when I mention a certain type of "channel" in this book and compare them with other types of "channels" or "customers."

THE CHANNEL

In a business model context[87] the channel is the way(s) we take[88] our products and services to our customers.

We basically have two options:

→ We can have a *direct* channel, where we command all the resources required on our own payroll.

→ We can use an *indirect* approach using various levels and types of *independent* channel partners.

In the software industry the term *channel* is often used to describe the situation where *independent third party* companies resell the software vendor's products to the final customer and technically[89]

---

[87] See the chapter Conceptual Framework.

[88] Promote, sell, extend, integrate, implement and support.

[89] According to the Business Model Generation framework.

speaking this is wrong. I recommend adopting the business model terminology and distinguish between a *direct* channel approach and an *indirect* channel approach. Just claiming that we use a channel doesn't explain if it is direct or indirect.

In order to comply with the business model definition the channel must promote *our* brand to the customers. The customers must perceive the software vendor as their "supplier" even though the delivery, the invoice and the support may be provided through an independent third party company.

If our brand is not visible to the reseller's customer, then the reseller is not our channel, but rather our final customer. Even if our revenue is tied to the revenue of our customer we do not consider her a channel partner if our brand is unknown to the customer's customer.

> *Why do we distinguish between indirect channels and customers?*

We do so because the relationship with an independent channel partner is completely different from the relationship with a customer. A channel partner lives from adding value to and reselling our stuff. She has an objective interest in selling as much as possible of our stuff and we can have an intelligent and joyful conversation with her regarding what it will take to sell even more.

A customer is using our stuff somewhere in her operation. She is interested in getting our stuff at the lowest price possible and she is not interested in our revenue and market leadership ambitions.

The conversations we have with our channel partners are completely different from the conversations we have with customers. The transactional motives of independent channel partners and customers are completely different.

There is a grey area and that is the White Label/OEM business and I will discuss this later in this Appendix.

BUSINESS PARTNER

Although the term "Business Partner" indicates some kind of partnership this is almost never the case when the term is used in the software industry. In the software industry the term Business Partner is used casually for any relationship where we work together as third parties each responsible for our own activities and our own P&L.

Throughout this book I use the term "independent channel partner" to emphasize that channel partners make their own business decisions based on their own ambitions and aspirations, their own business strategy and their own management capabilities. When we entertain a direct channel approach we can hire and fire people as required. We can set the direction of the business and we can manage the activities to comply with our ambitions and strategy. The direct and the indirect channel approach are like night and day. Motivating and managing people on our own payroll versus motivating and managing people on other's payrolls does not have much in common and that is why we claim to have a third party business model inside our own business model when we serve the market through independent channel partners.

ISV

The term Independent Software Vendor is used in the software industry for companies that develop their own software, which they take to the market under their own brand. ISVs will often use software components from other ISVs (or open source components) and thus become target customer segments for these ISVs.

Microsoft started out as an ISV selling to other ISVs. Apple sourced their first Basic compiler (with floating point integer) from Microsoft. None of Apple's customers were exposed to the Microsoft brand through this transaction and Apple did not pay Microsoft a royalty on each product they shipped to their customers. Therefore Apple was not a channel for Microsoft, but a customer. When Microsoft later made Office available for OS X and sold the licenses through Apple, then Apple became a Microsoft channel partner.

When ISVs are small with little brand awareness they may promote that their software runs on the components of more recognized ISVs (powered by Microsoft SQL, powered by SharePoint or powered by Oracle) even though they do not even resell these software components. However, as ISVs grow and gain more market awareness they will suppress the presence of third party components in their promotion. They will focus all their efforts on their own brand and invest in making themselves independent of other ISVs.

ISVs can also grow from within the large Value Added Reseller ecosystems. A Value Added Reseller[90] of SAP may have developed a vertical add-on solution, which she productizes and sells to other customers (potentially through other Value Added Resellers). This is an ISV activity, which is often co-branded with the software platform on which it depends.

Because Independent Software Vendors have a strong interest in promoting their own brands and suppress the brands of their suppliers they are not considered a "channel," but rather a customer segment in their own right. ISVs selling to other ISVs have a customer relationship when the buying ISV does not pay a price that is related to the revenue she generates.

ISVs selling to other ISVs have a channel relationship when the buying ISV does pay a price which is related to the revenue she generates AND the selling ISV's brand is transparent to the customer AND the customer can use the software from the first ISV independently of the

---

[90] See the section on Value Added Resellers

software from the second ISV. As you will conclude when reading the rest of this Appendix the second type of ISV is basically a Value Added Reseller.

You may find this explanation academic and it maybe overly complicated, but I can assure you that it is crucial to distinguish between a channel relationship and a customer relationship.

RESELLER

The reseller is typically "just" reselling the products of the ISVs to the customers.

The value of the reseller for the ISV is in marketing and sales making it easy for the customers to find the most appropriate product matching her needs and making it easy for the customer performing the purchase transactions.

Smaller ISVs, especially with standard products, go though resellers leaving them all the sales and marketing "hassle." The reseller marks up the price to cover her cost of sales and provide a profit margin. Although illegal in most countries, many ISVs operate with a Recommended Retail Price on which the reseller is granted a discount. The discount is typically between 30 and 40 per cent and the discount will grow with the increase in sales of the software.

Resellers often carry many complimentary and competing products ensuring that the customer acquisition cost is spread across as many revenue streams as possible and that the customer lifetime value is maximized.

VAR

A Value Added Reseller combines the software products from ISV's with her own services and her own and other products providing total solutions for her customers.

Initially the VAR has a clear interest promoting the brand of her ISV partners. As the VAR grows her business she may represent several competing ISVs and the ISV brand promotion may receive less attention compared to the promotion of the VAR's own brand. However, the VAR will always clearly communicate the support of her ISV brands when this is important to her customers as in the VAR domain the customers often choose the ISV brand first and the VAR second.

Because of the value add provided by the VAR the ISV can reach many more segments in the market without having to invest in product features and market communication for each and every segment. Thus with Value Added Resellers a software vendor can achieve a much wider reach as well as minimizing the risk of market over-penetration.

Value Added Resellers are more loyal to their ISVs than simple resellers due to the investment in skills and add-on solutions they make over time and the Value Added Reseller is the most beloved[91] indirect channel in the software industry.

Using a Value Added Reseller's channel requires a product that offers the value add opportunity, as well as having opportunities for developing add-on solutions, customizations and auxiliary services.

---

[91] In the research for this book I interviewed the CEO of the Scales Group, Hasse Bergman. The Scales Group is a Microsoft Dynamics AX VAR. Hasse told me that out of their total revenue only 10% comes from licenses and software maintenance contracts. 90% of their revenue is generated through professional services such as consulting, customization, integration, training and support. The Scales Group is a premium Dynamics AX VAR for Microsoft. They are extremely loyal and they secure long lasting relationships with their customers securing Microsoft add-on business and software maintenance revenue.

DISTRIBUTOR

The definition of a distributor is someone who recruits and manages resellers on behalf of the ISV.

The software market was created by personal computers from Apple and IBM and in the early years of the software market products were delivered in shrink-wrapped boxes with the software on floppy disks and loads of printed documentation. Software products needed physical logistics to get to the customers. A structure with a distributor and resellers worked well serving consumers and business customers and distributors with a large network of resellers were really valuable to ISVs.

With the introduction of the Internet everything changed.

With the ability to deliver the product and the documentation electronically through the Internet the need for the distributor's warehouses and logistic capabilities disappeared. With the ability for customers to search and find the ISVs and communicate directly, the need for the distributor as a logistics and also as a communication channel disappeared.

The traditional distributor is a dying breed in the software industry and is being replaced by app stores and software publishers.

VAD

A Value Added Distributor is an independent third party company serving the Reseller, VAR and Systems Integrator community with products from ISVs and the associated services required for successful market management. The Value Added Distributor is essentially acting on behalf of the ISV, and the emphasis of the VAD is not on the logistics of distribution, but on the market development and management services they provide. The VAD undertakes branding activities, recruits resellers, trains the reseller's staff and manages the resellers according to the guidelines provided by the ISV.

The large ISVs such as Oracle, SAP, Microsoft, Adobe etc. all have subsidiaries in most countries in the world. They all directly provide the services required to recruit and manage the partner channel and to manage the market in general, but every now and again, they will also engage with Value Added Distributors.

Smaller ISVs may not have the financial capacity to open their own subsidiaries fast enough and have a strong incentive to assign the market development and management responsibilities to a VAD. Some markets may be too small to set up dedicated subsidiaries and it then makes sense for the ISV to assign his representation responsibilities to a local VAD.

As distributors are dying Value Added Distributors are growing. There is a huge need for Value Added Distributors in the smaller markets, but also in larger markets helping new ISVs to get started from scratch.

OEM AND WHITE LABELING

White Labeling means taking the product of an ISV to the market under a different label. The customer will believe that the product originates from the white labeling party and will not recognize the ISV as the originator of the product.

An Original Equipment Manufacturer will source components from ISVs, embed them in her own products and take the full package to the market under her own brand, thus the suppliers to an OEM are invisible to the customers of the OEM.

Only very powerful suppliers such as Intel and Microsoft can enforce an "xx inside" branding policy. Most other suppliers will have to live with the anonymity in the final product and unless the ISV can get his label on the cover of the PC or maintain his own brand vis-à-vis the customer White Labels and OEMs are clearly not a Channel, but customer segments in their own right.

I allow that they are not typical customers in so far as our sales to them are a function of their sales to their customers. However, their customers are not our customers and our products enjoy no brand affinity; they don't even know that we exist.

I often have heated discussions with my colleagues in the software industry on the nature of white labeling and OEM relationships. I consider OEM and white labeling relationships as customer relationships and not channel relationships. I disqualify OEM and white labeling parties as partners because they do not carry my brand to the customers. With OEM and white labeling parties I cannot build brand awareness with their customers. I cannot become the leading player in any market segment though OEM and white labeling because I am - and remain - completely unknown. Thus OEM and White Labels become my customers and not my channel.

SALES AGENT

A Sales Agent is an independent third party company (often just a single person) representing the ISV in the sales activities aimed at winning customers or recruiting channel partners for the ISV's products. Very often the Sales Agent is already well established in the market segment in question with good connections to potential customers and channel partners. In this respect the Sales Agent acts more as an intermediary or a broker as his main interest is maintaining his good relationships with the potential customers and channel partners rather than with the ISVs who come and go.

In other industries the Sales Agent typically works on commission only, but with long sales cycles this remuneration concept doesn't work well in the software industry. Here the Sales Agent typically works with a fixed monthly retainer, activity based bonuses, a commission on sales accomplished and reimbursement of expenses.

Are Sales Agents channel partners?

No. In the software industry Sales Agents typically represent the ISV (often with a business card pretending that she is on the payroll of that ISV) and the final commercial relationship is always between the ISV and the customer.

In markets with only a few, but large deals, ISV's may be represented by Sales Agents on a long term basis, otherwise Sales Agents are primarily engaged by smaller ISV's who cannot afford to hire their own sales people in a new market.

SYSTEMS INTEGRATOR

A Systems Integrator works on behalf of customers helping them integrate, implement and manage IT systems. Officially there is no formal relationship between ISVs and Systems Integrators. The software used by the customer is not acquired though the Systems Integrators, but through other sources. If a Systems Integrator delivers products to her customers then she by definition becomes a Value Added Reseller.

This definition may seem tortuous, but there is a substantial difference between being a Value Added Reseller and being a Systems Integrator. The Systems Integrator is supposed to be working exclusively for the customer. The customer expects that the Systems Integrator is independent of economic interests with third parties. The Systems Integrator cannot maintain her independent status if she has a vested interest in selling software on which she receives a margin.

Systems Integrators are not channel partners, but rather a group of companies that have an indirect influence on the decision making process with certain customer segments and that are critical for delivering the auxiliary services required for project success.

What we consider Systems Integrators in the real world are often a combination of the ISV, VAR and Systems Integrator roles. There is no law against reselling someone's software, developing your own software and integrating other people's software within the walls of the same company and many of the biggest Systems Integrators in the software industry now perform hybrids of all these roles.

SUBSIDIARY

A subsidiary is a fully owned (by the mother company) operation responsible for certain business activities. Subsidiaries are fully controlled by their mother companies and thus represent the most direct and effective way of implementing a global strategy. However, they are expensive to establish and run and they also require a corresponding management infrastructure at the headquarter level.

All the large ISVs have global subsidiaries taking care of their business interests irrespective of whether they have a direct or an indirect channel approach to the market.

Large VARs, System Integrators, VADs etc. also have a headquarter/subsidiary format for their global operations.

Any company in the software industry affected by local representation must at some stage be prepared to establish a headquarter/subsidiary infrastructure if they have ambitions for assuming positions as global market leaders.

Joint Venture

A Joint Venture is a business setup with two or more parties sharing the investments, management and P&L of an operation.

In the software industry front office Joint Ventures are often an intermediate step when moving into a new territory where the incoming party brings the product and the local party brings the infrastructure needed to accelerate market penetration and management.

Joint Ventures are not very popular in the software industry. Although Joint Ventures in theory offer many benefits, they are difficult to establish and operate when the timing of the results are hard to predict. As the outcome of the penetration of new markets by default is very hard to predict, most companies prefer to appoint an exclusive Value Added Distributor in a new market and then acquire this distributor when the time is right for a direct representation.

Franchise

The franchise format so popular in many industries has never made any substantial inroad into the software industry.

The format operates with the Franchisee who faces the customers and the Franchisor who holds the intellectual property rights to the products and business processes. The Franchisee acquires a license allowing her access to a Franchisor's proprietary knowledge, processes and trademarks in order to allow her to sell a product or provide a service under the Franchisor's brand name. In exchange for gaining the franchise, the Franchisee usually pays the Franchisor an initial start-up fee and recurring licensing fees related to performance.

The main reason for the lack of success in the software industry is the traditional focus on the products and much less on the processes required to find, win and make happy customers (the value chain).

ISVs have typically not been able to, or have expressed little interest in productizing the business processes required to drive the full value chain.

I believe we will see many more Franchise models in the software industry in the future. As the products become more and more alike and it becomes steadily easier to catch up on functionality, the processes around the products becomes much more important. The emphasis will shift from the product itself to the processes associated with finding, winning, making, keeping and growing happy customers. Getting "best practice" approaches implemented fast becomes a critical path to market leadership. As building subsidiaries fast is extremely capital intensive and risky, the Franchise approach offers an attractive alternative, where the Franchisee has a clear upside as opposed to the salaried country manager. I think we will see the Franchise model introduced at the VAD level first and then on the VAR/Reseller level next.

MASTER FRANCHISE

A Master Franchise represents the Franchisor and is responsible for recruiting and managing Franchisees in a specific geographic market.

APPENDIX B

This Appendix includes an in-depth review of the methodology and vocabulary that will help us build powerful partner channels if and when that route to market is available.

THE BUSINESS MODEL

Alexander Osterwalder and Yves Pigneur published the book Business Model Generation[92] in 2010. The book is primarily based on Osterwalder's research (Ph.D. dissertation). In the span of just a few years the business model canvas and the formats used by Osterwalder and Pigneur have spread like wildfire all over the world. Osterwalder and Pigneur didn't invent the concept of "the business model," but they provided a precise and consistent definition and made the concept comprehensible and operational.

---

[92] Osterwalder, Alexander, Yves Pigneur, and Tim Clark. 2010. Business model generation : a handbook for visionaries, game changers, and challengers (Wiley: Hoboken, NJ).

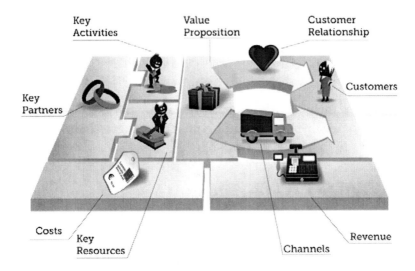

Figure 20: The business model canvas.

With the business model canvas we see the big picture instantly. Yes, this is a 360-degree depiction of a business! The small graphical icons support our immediate understanding and our ability to memorize the picture. It takes just 28 pages to describe the nine building blocks that make up the business model. Each of the pages is rich on graphics and is segmented into short paragraphs. Compared to most other business books we are in a completely different and much more comprehensible universe.

VALUE PROPOSITIONS

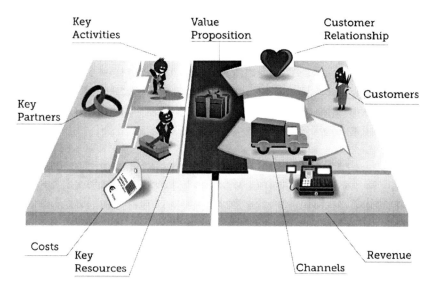

Figure 21: The customer value proposition is much more than just the product.

We have a come a long way from the day where we talked primarily about our products and services to the present day where we first and foremost talk about *value propositions*[93]. The value propositions are obviously based on the products and services we provide to our customers, but instead of focusing on the features and functions of our products and services we translate these features and functions into the benefits and value they create for our customers.

When Geoffrey Moore published his famous book "Crossing the Chasm[94]" in 1991 he also coined the concept of "the whole product" as the combination of products and services required for a customer to get the full benefit/value of our products and/or services.

The software industry is full of business models where there is a major difference between the product/service and "the whole

---

[93] Osterwalder, Alexander, Yves Pigneur, Gregory Bernarda, and Alan Smith. 2014. Value proposition design : how to create products and services customers want.

[94] Moore, Geoffrey A. 2014. Crossing the chasm : marketing and selling disruptive products to mainstream customers (HarperBusiness, an imprint of HarperCollins Publishers: New York, NY).

product." Just think of business process optimization software that is worthless without business process standardization, implementation, customization, integration, training and support. As this book is focusing on Level 2-3 value-add type software companies the value propositions are always very different from the virtues of our products and includes such items as domain focus, insight and experience, customer testimonials, consulting and implementation capabilities, solidity and market position.

The purpose of our value proposition is to explain to our ideal customers the great value we can provide compared to their alternatives[95] and the low risk that choosing us represents. Level 2-3 software companies always need two layers in their customer value propositions:

+ The GENERIC customer value proposition is the position we take when communicating to the market. This value proposition will help all potential customers understand what they can expect from us.

+ The SPECIFIC customer value proposition is designed for the individual customer as we engage in the specific project learning which exact objectives that our customer is pursuing.

When we choose to find, win, make, keep and grow happy customers through independent channel partners, we then need to complement our customer value proposition(s) with *partner* value propositions. The independent channel partners may be excited about, but are never motivated to invest in the partnership by the virtues of our products per se. They are motivated by the opportunity to build a profitable *business* with and around our products. The partner value proposition explains this opportunity and how we help make that happen. Only the making of many successful partners will make

---

[95] Technically the competitive perspective is covered in the business model environment analysis.

us successful. Alas, the responsibility for making our independent partner channel successful remains on our shoulders.

With the declining cost of making software and with the increased transparency provided by the Internet, there are more software companies with products looking for independent channel partners than there are independent channel partners looking for software companies with products. Making it to market leadership with an indirect channel approach therefore requires very powerful customer and partner value propositions.

Once we have recruited the partners we then need to understand their customer value propositions and more often than not we even have to help them craft targeted and powerful value propositions, because that is fundamental for success in the market, but unfortunately also very difficult for most marketers.

CUSTOMER SEGMENTS

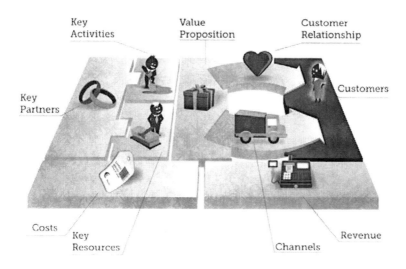

Figure 22: Market segmentation is crucial for all software companies and leaving this exercise to the independent channel partner represents both a risk and an opportunity.

Who are our ideal customers?

Do we even have to ask that question if we pass the responsibility for marketing and sales (and more) to independent channel partners?

I have several examples of independent channel partners who have mis-positioned a B2B software product in the market. The agony of dealing with unhappy resellers and customers is time consuming and the damage to the brand can be very high as rumors and the industry news media pick up on unhappy customer experiences. Where independent channel partners may extend our market reach they may also bring our products to segments in the market where there is a very poor fit. Partners may push hard on us to retroactively provide this fit because they are comfortable in this segment, and the customers, who have acquired our product and experience inconveniences will do the same.

The risk for SAP, Oracle, Microsoft, IBM, and other big software companies of partners mis-positioning their product is negligible, but for the start-up and smaller software company it can be downright devastating. When we only have tiny market shares and only entertain a few partners, their mistakes will reflect back on us. That is not the case when we are a Level 3 mature mode company with solid market shares and hundreds or thousands of partners.

Precise market segmentation and identification of the ideal customers are critically important on the path to global market leadership in the software industry when we choose the independent channel partner approach.

We have to be very precise in defining our ideal customer profiles and work very closely with our independent channel partners helping them understand where they should focus their sales and marketing efforts. This focus on carefully selected customer segments is crucial, especially in the early days of our path to market leadership. The faster we can claim and be recognized as the market leader in a certain segment the sooner we will be caught by Geoffrey Moore's proverbial tornado. In the tornado we don't need to worry about getting customers, but "only" to worry about building demand fulfillment capacity and that is a wonderful problem to wrestle with.

As a Level 2-3 mature mode type software company we deliberately want to make sure that our channel partners do not target the exact same customers. As we grow the number of partners we will first and foremost be concerned with ensuring geographical market coverage. The channel partner that we first sign up in a geographic market will enjoy her solitude and be somewhat concerned when we appoint the second channel partner. Unless we work hand-in-hand with the channel partners, targeting more precise sub-segments of our total market they will start to feel that we are over-penetrating as we appoint the third, forth, fifth, sixth partner, etc.

We need to keep in mind that channel partners very seldom share our ambitions for market leadership. The vast majority of channel partners just want to run a profitable and stable business that they can manage. Being alone in the market representing a recognized brand is the ultimate comfort position of most channel partners. With few exceptions we need to help the channel partners with narrowing their focus on smaller sub-segments where they can build and enjoy a strong position.

CHANNELS

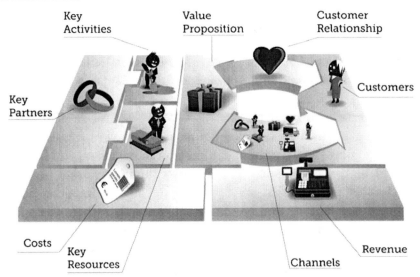

Figure 23: The indirect channel is a third party business model in our own business model.

The Channel is the choices we make for how to find, win, make, keep and grow happy customers. The word "channel" is typically used in the software industry to describe independent companies that assume various roles and obligations in bringing a software product to the customers. The definition is rather broad, since the roles and obligations can vary substantially from "simple" reselling to systems integration, solution development on top of our software, implementation in terms of consulting, project management, customization, training and support.

In order to comply with the business model terminology we should distinguish between the *direct* channel approach and the indirect channel approach.

The direct channel approach means employing our own sales, marketing and support resources and deploying them in the activities aimed at finding, winning, making, keeping and growing happy customers.

The indirect channel approach means contracting with independent third party companies that employ their own development, product management, marketing, sales and support resources and deploy them in the activities aimed at finding, winning, making, keeping and growing happy customers (for them and us).

Thus looking at the business model from the perspective of a Level 2-3 value-add software company the independent channel partners become much more than just a marketing and sales channel. The channel partners form an eco-system that enables us to reach much further than we could ever do on our own. No company in any industry on the planet can accomplish the same alone as they can accomplish cooperating with external partners and in the software industry independent channel partners not only extend the simple penetration, but extend and complement our value proposition reaching into corners of the market that we would never be able to reach alone.

Many software companies behave as if they "own" their independent resellers and can command the ways they should operate. This perception and the associated behavior is one of the main root causes for failure with an indirect channel in the software industry. The independent channel partners are independent enterprises with independent ambitions, personalities, backgrounds, beliefs, strategies, value propositions and P&L. They may be specialized small and medium sized owner-managed companies or they may be medium and large enterprises with hired management and a broad line of products and services. Each and everyone has their own agenda and issues and do not consider themselves our channel! They know that we define them as our channel partners, but they obviously strive to stay as independent as possible minimizing the risk associated with our choice of strategy and behavior. In the business model terminology our independent channel partners consider their software vendors their *key partners*, i.e a part of their business model back office.

When using the business model terminology we also avoid the mistake of considering the independent channel partners as our customers or our non-salaried marketing, sales, pre-sales, implementation and support staff. I still hear software company executives making such statements and as I mentioned above nothing could be more misleading. Channel partners are building their businesses around reselling our products. They are not "consuming" our product. The business models of the channel partners are completely different from our own business models as software companies. Channel Partners are not attracted primarily by our product and our customer value proposition, but by the business that our product can enable and facilitate for their business model.

> *The business model of a software company and the business model of her independent channel partners are not identical. While we are a Key Partner in her business model she is an Independent Channel Partner in our business model.*

CUSTOMER RELATIONSHIPS

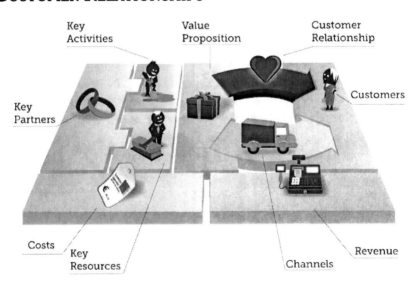

Figure 24: The introduction of independent channel partners doesn't mean that we should give up all our relationships with the customers.

This business model building block defines how we best interact with our customers to achieve the highest possible level of customer satisfaction as well as optimizing the revenue streams from and profitability of our value propositions over the lifetime of the relationships[96]. In this corner of the business model we are concerned with keeping churn down and maximizing customer lifetime value.

I deliberately use the term *"our customers."* Although most software companies using the indirect channel approach over time will leave many of the customer relationship activities to their channel partners, we should still consider the customers our customers. If and when the customer gets unsatisfied with her partner we should be able to accommodate the shift to another partner without losing the customer to one of our competitors.

The path to global market leadership goes through building a brand. Although our partners may create most of the total value delivered to our customers we want to make sure that the customers maintain affinity to our brand and not only to the brand of the individual channel partner.

The one relationship a software company should never ever leave to their channel partners is the license[97] relationship. The right to use the software should be passed directly from the software company to the end user. Not only in legal terms, which is always the case, but also in practical terms. Thus a software company should know ALL their licensees. This fundamental principle also applies for Software-as-a-Service and Cloud-based delivery formats.

When software companies use the indirect channel approach their customer relationships typically become impersonal and unilateral. Customers may receive email newsletters from the principal and they

---

[96] Often called Customer Lifetime Value

[97] Or a subscription relationship for the "software-as-a-service" delivery format.

may subscribe to her Twitter and other social media updates and we will typically maintain a one-to-many communication approach to our customers. However, we need to provide the customers with an easy path to reach out to us if they are not pleased with their current channel partner and want another one.

Many software companies keep track of the level of customer satisfaction and use this metric to rate the status of their independent channel partners and this certainly makes sense. Happy customers are the most secure path to getting and retaining market leadership and we don't want to lose control of this lever.

To support our product management function we also need direct relationships with customers from whom we can learn what should be included or changed in the core products in future releases. We cannot afford to only listen to the independent channel partners and how they interpret what we should develop and what we should leave the channel to provide.

REVENUE

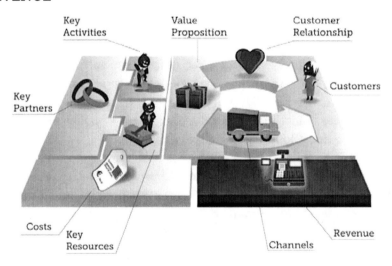

Figure 25: When we use independent channel partners then we will also give up all the auxiliary revenue streams.

Our efforts in selling our value propositions to our customers should generate revenue. The revenue sources can be plentiful including licenses, subscriptions, consulting, training, project management, customization, integration, software engineering etc. The software industry is rich on business models where the software may be the core product, but in many cases the auxiliary services generate the biggest revenue and gross margin provider[98] in the business model.

As mentioned above, the revenue streams from auxiliary products can often be financially greater and more numerous than the revenue from the software itself and this is a challenge as well as an opportunity. When the software itself is just a minor part of the whole product, then there is an attractive value creation opportunity for the independent channel partners. However, the learning curve is then correspondingly long and steep for new channel partners.

When there is only limited auxiliary revenue streams associated with a software product, then the learning curve for new independent channel partners is short and flat. On the other hand the long term potential is less attractive and the product less sticky. Products that are easy to take on-board, from the view of an independent channel partner, are also easy to replace.

For Level 2-3 value-add software companies using independent channel partners to find, win, make, keep and grow happy customers means leaving a portion of the product revenue and most of the auxiliary revenue to the partners. The more revenue a product can generate for a channel partner the more interesting the business opportunity will be in the long run.

---

[98] Since the introduction of the Internet the software industry has fostered the so called double-sided business models. Facebook, Google and Twitter are good examples of such business models where the users do not pay anything for the service, but the revenue is generated by advertisers or other parties interested in communicating with the users. This book primarily deals with single sided business models where the users and the customers are the same.

As our only source of revenue comes from the software[99] we have to carefully manage how we share this revenue stream with our channel partners. Initially, channel partners focus heavily on the margin they receive from us, but as the relationship develops they learn that the key to profitability is in the auxiliary services. Margins are like staff salaries; a hygiene factor that may cause dissatisfaction, but on the other hand does not generate changes in behavior. We can use different levels of margins to stimulate certain behavior, such as providing higher margins for higher volumes of sales, but as revenue for Level 2-3 value-add software companies is project driven rather than product driven and as our share of the project revenue is fairly small, then the level of margin will only have minor motivational impact on the behavior of our channel partners.

I therefore recommend Level 2-3 value-add software companies to keep the margin they pass to their independent channel partner as low as possible and motivate with other incentives and support activities that steer the partners in the direction we want them to take.

Do we generate revenue from the independent channel partners, which is not coming from the customers?

Yes we do, but that should be considered a cost relief rather than genuine revenue.

We will charge for training, certification, partner events and we may even charge a fixed recurring membership fee in exchange for access to our channel partner platforms. Charging the independent channel partners for these services makes good sense. If the services we provide have value then they should also have a price tag. The cost relief will enable us to provide more and better services and it will force us to ensure the quality of the services, but it should never constitute a primary revenue source.

---

[99] Delivered in the traditional perpetual up-front pre-paid license format or as a recurring subscription charge.

Our ability to charge for non-revenue related services such as training and certification always depends on the power balance between the channel partners and us. If the channel partner has a huge foot-print in the market that we would like to access, then she will obviously use this position to negotiate favorable terms and conditions with us. We will be tempted to offer customized terms and conditions motivated by the sales volume expected later on. However, that may never materialize. There is no guarantee that large organizations will actually perform well. My own experience is that it takes major effort to make large organizations perform well for us. Unless there is a committed and enthusiastic top executive driving the effort then the sheer inertia of large organizations is more likely to consume our scarce partner account management resources than generate any significant business for us.

KEY RESOURCES

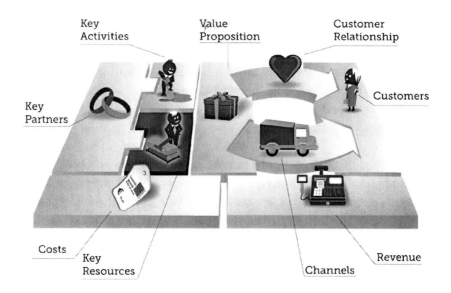

Figure 26: The key resources in the software industry are people and those required for managing the indirect partner channel are very different from those required for serving the customers directly.

The key resources in the software industry are money and people and the only[100] thing you can do with the money is hire more and better people.

Software companies are very fortunate. Compared to most other industries the software industry is extremely fixed-asset light. Starting a software company requires people, computers, software and data communication networks. There is no need for exploration underground, laboratories, 0-series, molding tools, inventories, FDA approval, factories, trucks etc. Starting a software company may require less investment than starting as a hairdresser. On the other hand, the software industry is cursed by the invisibility of their products and an enormous influx of new companies. Communicating the virtues of software products requires smart marketing and sales people (best of all is a long list of happy customers).

The nature of the marketing, sales and support resources needed are directly related to the customer value proposition and to the choice of channel. Selling directly to customers is completely different from recruiting and managing channel partners, who then in turn assume responsibility for finding, winning, making, keeping and growing happy customers. Choosing to serve the market through an indirect channel of independent partners will create a need for resources to recruit, support and manage these partners. I cannot emphasize enough the fact that *the skill sets required to find, win, make, keep and grow happy customers are not the same skill sets required to find, win, make and keep productive independent channel partners.* Happy customers and productive partners are two very different objectives and if we take the indirect channel route then we need to master both! Choosing a go-to-market approach based on independent channel partners requires additional resources and skills in our organization compared to the direct approach. We still need to fully understand the entire business model including how and why our customers should

---

[100] There are obviously also other operational and promotion expenses, but most of them are associated with the number of people we employ.

prefer and acquire our products, but in addition we now also need to understand how to operate our business model through independent channel partners and we need the resources and skills required to find, recruit, enable and grow these partners.

If we didn't originally develop our value proposition based on serving the market through independent channel partners, then we may have to redesign our products to make them more attractive for the partners. Simply taking a business model based on a direct channel approach and replacing the channel will not work unless we re-engineer the rest of the business model including the value propositions.

I often come across software companies that are unsuccessful with their direct channel based business model believing that by changing the channel they will become successful. I can almost guarantee that without a major business model reengineering this approach will fail. The key resources are closely related to the all the building blocks in the front-office of our business model, thus changing the channel approach requires changes to the key resources also.

Key Activities

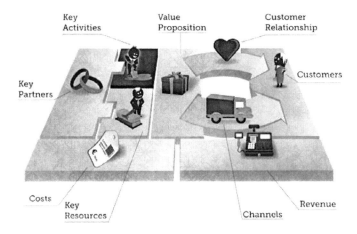

Figure 27: The key activities associated with managing indirect partner channels are very different from those associated with serving the customers.

To run a software company your Key Resources must plan and execute certain Key Activities in order to produce more revenue than cost and thus generate a profit.

Again, the software industry is very fortunate.

Other industries have to carefully manage their supply chains ensuring that they have neither too much nor too little supply available to meet future demand. Industries dealing with physical products need to manage field engineering changes to already shipped products and some industries have to manage spare parts and obtain FDA approval.

Most of the companies in the software industry don't need to worry about such critical, time consuming and expensive issues.

A software company must master just three major activities:

A. Develop and support products and services that customers really need and want.

B. Sell these products and services at a price generating enough gross margin cost to cover the fixed R&D, admin and sales/marketing cost.

C. Support these products ensuring customers stay and grow.

When a software company chooses to approach the market through independent channel partners they will need to master a fourth set of activities:

D. Find, recruit, enable and grow productive partners.

*Will the choice of approaching the market through
independent channel partners make the need for
category B type activities obsolete?*

No. If we have no practical experience with what it takes to sell and support our software to the customers, then we will not be able to recruit the right partners and manage them successfully. This wasn't the case 20 years ago, but today the software industry has matured. The independent channel partner landscape has become much more professional and expects the software vendors to provide much more than just a competitive product. Software companies that choose to serve the market through independent channel partners must understand the full value chain of their business AND must have a framework for finding, winning, making and growing successful independent channel partners.

The activities required for finding, recruiting, enabling and growing productive partners are substantially different from the activities required for finding, winning, making, keeping and growing happy customers. We need to master and execute both sets of activities for at least the first 10-15 years as we help our independent channel partners become successful. We need to maintain solid lead generation activities that feed the channel with potential sales opportunities and we need to coach the sales process ensuring that the deals get closed and the partners learn how to do business with our product.

Our independent channel partners expect to know our plans for the future and they expect us to listen to their complaints and suggestions. Working through an indirect channel requires that we be much more structured in our product support, planning and release processes. With an indirect channel the product management function becomes a much more critical cog between the market and our R&D resources.

Selecting the indirect approach adds layers of complexity to our business model and demands additional resources, skills and activities. The payoff comes later in the form of the potential multiplication lever when we have demonstrated that we can actually find, recruit, enable and grow these partners on a global scale.

KEY PARTNERS (SUPPLIERS)

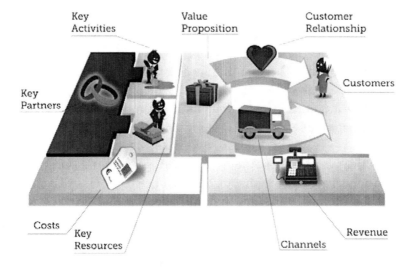

Figure 28: Software companies have few key partners and our independent channel partners are not in this category.

In the business model terminology our independent channel partners are not our key partners. In the business model terminology key partners are primarily suppliers that help us operate the business model back office.

In most other industries the supply chains are extremely critical. Companies rely on their suppliers and when suppliers fail companies fail. That is very seldom the case in the software industry and most Level 2-3 value-add software companies do not have any key partners at all.

If we are operating within the ecosystem of one of the big Level 2-3 software companies (Oracle, SAP, Microsoft, Autodesk etc.) then we will obviously have them as our key partners and whatever they decide may have a profound impact on our business and therefore we obviously follow them closely. However, the Level 2-3 software companies are also developing their software using standard development tools and seldom have intimate relationships with their vendors.

Our independent channel partners have us as their key partner and we will work hard to make that dependency as strong as possible (we call it loyalty!). On the other hand our independent channel partners are not our key partners and we will work hard to avoid any dependency. We do not want to rely on the success of any single channel partner as that is fundamentally beyond our control.

In other industries the "key partners" play vital roles in extending the capabilities of the principals and the management of suppliers is often a key competence in such industries. That is not the case in the Level 2-3 software industry, where principals do not have any, or very few "key partners."

COST

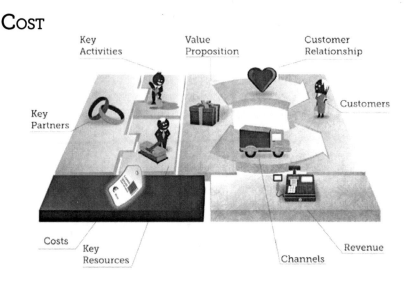

Figure 29: Software companies have cost of development and cost of sales, but hardly any costs associated with production. The migration to a cloud based delivery format introduces substantial cost of operation although the marginal cost is still very small compared to other industries.

The business model "back office" creates cost and again the software industry is very different from most industries. The software industry has fixed capacity costs and almost no variable costs.

The marginal cost of producing an additional copy of a software product or adding an extra subscriber to a SaaS service is very close to zero. However, the auxiliary services required for implementing the software may have considerable variable cost. This phenomenon explains why many software companies start out with a direct channel approach where they enjoy the revenue stream generated by the auxiliary services, which often help sponsor the initial development of the software. The developers typically deliver the services in the early days of the life of a software company and as time passes the development is separated from support and implementation, which then become separate profit centers.

Software companies with considerable support and implementation requirements have a very hard time changing their business models from a direct channel approach to an indirect channel approach. Imagine that we provide software-based solutions where the software revenue represents 25% of total revenue. We consider introducing the indirect channel approach and our partner value proposition looks attractive since the partners are to provide the service portion. Let's assume that we need to provide the independent channel partner with a 40% discount on the list price. Shifting to the indirect channel approach will then leave us with only 15%[101] of the revenue from each deal compared to the situation where we delivered directly. Making this shift will require investment in resources and activities needed for finding, recruiting, enabling and growing these partners on a global scale. How soon will these investments pay off?

One of the most important cost elements in the Level 2-3 value-add software industry is the Customer Acquisition Cost. Finding, winning and making new customers may be a lengthy and thus expensive process. Enterprise and SMB customers in the market for software solutions with big price tags and of strategic and operational importance will run decision making processes involving committees of stakeholders and external consultants. The vendors will have to go through a series of demos, workshops and tests before the final choice is made.

When we shift from a direct channel to an indirect channel we will have to perform the activities and employ the resources to master channel recruitment and management as well as stand side by side with the partners mastering the direct sales process. Thus such a shift requires major investments for a number of years before we have channel partners that can perform on their own and we can enjoy the extended reach and multiplication rewards.

---

[101] You get 60% of 50% = 30%

THE BUSINESS MODEL ENVIRONMENT

When we take a close look at the business model canvas we notice the absence of some significant areas impacting upon our business. Where do we deal with the competition, the technology trends, the legal and environmental issues, the global economy, culture etc. etc.? No business model lives in a vacuum and the toughest part in business is actually dealing with the issues that we cannot control.

The business model environment represents all the parameters and variables that we cannot control. The business model environment will expose us to risk factors that we must mitigate, but also to opportunities that we can and should take advantage of. Applying the business model framework, but ignoring the business model environment is not going to work well.

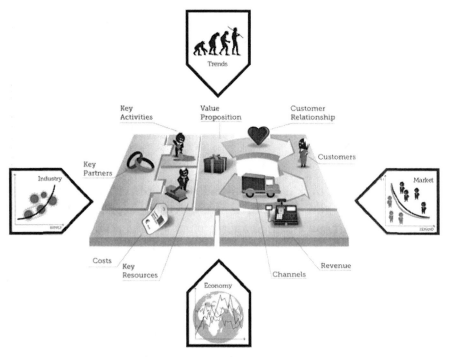

Figure 31: The business model environment, representing all the factors that we do not control, should not be ignored.

The business model environment is divided into four[102] major areas:

1. KEY TRENDS
2. MARKET FORCES
3. INDUSTRY FORCES
4. MACRO ECONOMIC FORCES

Osterwalder's four business model environment forces are fairly comprehensive and complete and will work well for most software driven companies when used in a channel development context.

Working with our independent channel partners we will spend considerable time discussing the business model environment and it becomes paramount that we have a shared framework helping us with the analysis and with making operational conclusions. Osterwalder's business model environment framework can be learned and implemented in a 1-day workshop and will also help us to distinguish between prejudices, assumptions and facts, which is required when we recruit and ramp-up new channel partners and when we develop growth strategies with current partners.

KEY TRENDS

THE KEY TRENDS INCLUDE:

1. TECHNOLOGY TRENDS
2. REGULATORY TRENDS
3. SOCIETAL & CULTURAL TRENDS
4. SOCIOECONOMIC TRENDS

---

[102] Osterwalder actually names these areas "forces", which in my opinion may confuse them with Porter's "Five Forces" to which there is some, but not complete, overlap. http://www.exed.hbs.edu/assets/documents/hbr-shape-strategy.pdf

Most software-driven business models receive substantial impact from the Key Trends forces. Actually the software driven industry is the main technology driver in itself, and combined the industry has more impact on the business model environment forces than most other industries.

The rapid proliferation of the Internet, the standardization of digital media formats, the acceptance of smart personal mobile computers (smart phones and tablets), the "invention" of apps and apps ecosystems, the development of the "cloud", the availability of in-memory analytical tools, the Internet of things, etc., etc., are all technology drivers enabling some companies' business models to grow and scale rapidly while completely disrupting other companies' business models.

Many business model environment issues are of a global nature, but as we move into new geographies the local legal, culture, language, and market requirements may have a profound impact on our own business model elements as well as on the business model elements of our local channel partners.

MARKET FORCES

In the business model terminology the market represents our customers (current and potential), their organizations, the media serving them, the consultants helping them and other demand side stakeholders.

THE MARKET FORCES INCLUDE:

    1.   MARKET ISSUES

    2.   MARKET SEGMENTS

3.   NEEDS & DEMANDS

4.   SWITCHING COST

5.   REVENUE ATTRACTIVENESS

Although market forces also change over time, the main consideration here is the nature of our potential customers' situation, needs and behavior associated with their purchase and decision making process for our type of product/service.

When we consider if we should take the direct or indirect route to market, then we need to look to the market forces first, because if the value added by the indirect channel isn't recognized by the potential customers, then it will be hard to implement and scale our business model. Are there circumstances in the demand side of the market that speaks in favor of applying an indirect channel approach? What value and benefits will our customers get from being served indirectly by independent channel partners rather than by us directly? If we don't have the answers at hand we may have to get out of the building and talk to some potential customers to hear what they have to say on these issues. If there is little or no value to our customers by being served by independent channel partners then we have a poor case for choosing this route.

As we recruit and ramp-up partners we will have the exact same type of discussion when looking for growth opportunities for the individual partner, where these do not collide directly with those of other partners in the same area. Although we cannot and should not tell our channel partners which strategy to choose we can help by providing market intelligence and observations.

INDUSTRY FORCES

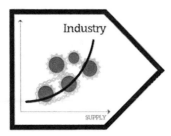

In the business model terminology the industry forces primarily represent our competitors, our potential channel partners, our industry organizations, the media serving us, the consultants helping us and other "supply side" stakeholders.

THE INDUSTRY FORCES INCLUDE:

1. COMPETITORS (INCUMBENTS)

2. NEW ENTRANTS (INSURGENTS)

3. SUBSTITUTE PRODUCTS & SERVICES

4. STAKEHOLDERS

5. SUPPLIERS & OTHER VALUE CHAIN ACTORS

When we consider choosing the indirect channel approach the industry forces also play a major role. How do our competitors operate? Is there a competitor dominating the position we want to take? Is there an indirect channel for what we provide or will we have to build the channel from scratch? Tapping into an existing channel is obviously a major advantage while building the channel first is extremely difficult.

While the role of our channel partners is to serve the customers directly, we will spend lots of time discussing competition, substitution options and other value chain actors (strategic alliances) with our potential channel partners. In the Level 1 channel development stage where we are still an unknown brand and need to recruit many new channel partners, they will rely heavily on the competitive analyses that we provide because they expect us to have the big overview. Making it into the reports[103] of the industry analysts is extremely important, giving potential channel partners as well as their potential customers an independent assessment of our position and ability to execute.

MACRO ECONOMIC FORCES

THE MACRO ECONOMIC FORCES INCLUDE:

1. GLOBAL MARKET CONDITIONS

2. CAPITAL MARKETS

3. COMMODITIES AND OTHER RESOURCES

4. ECONOMIC INFRASTRUCTURE

It certainly makes sense to look at the global Macro Economic Forces[104] when designing our business model to check if there are long-term trends that we can take advantage of or that will represent threats. However, I don't see this force having much impact on our choice of channel approach.

The software industry itself differs from most other industries by having a very slim supply side. As the main resource associated with developing software is people and as the marginal cost of producing software is close to zero, the industry is only slightly affected by changes in the Macro Economic Forces. Yes, on the demand side customers will be more reluctant in making investments when times

---

[103] Such as the Magic Quadrants from Gartner.

[104] I often hear executives from small software companies engage in macro economic speculation as the basis for selecting new markets. In my opinion this makes absolutely no sense. We'll never get our predictions right anyway and there are other critical issues such as customers, partners and competitors we need to deal with first.

are tough, but where companies invest in capacity expansion when times are good they also invest in cost reductions when times are tough, and it may involve the exact same software solutions.

It is also impossible to predict when and where times will be tough and I cannot recommend applying the gold digger mentality[105] and rushing to where the macro economic analysts predict the growth will move in the next 3-5 years. The predictions are mostly inaccurate and the changes happen so quickly that it makes our lives miserable constantly adjusting. In any case, building and managing market leadership directly or indirectly has a much longer perspective than the macro economic trends.

Also, the discussions we have with our channel partners will only be slightly affected by the macro economic forces. That many business people tend to blame their misfortune on the market, the industry or the macroeconomic trends doesn't necessarily mean that there is such a cause and effect relationship. Macro economic forces are very hard to predict, so we are typically better off dealing with issues as they materialize.

MANAGING THE BUSINESS MODEL ENVIRONMENT

While the entire business model environment is important when designing our global business model, I recommend focusing on the market and industry issues when considering the choice of channel.

No individual alone in our organization can paint a holistic picture of our business model's environment and design space. Only by mapping out each specialist's knowledge can we develop a shared understanding of our environment. Although there is nothing in the business model and business model environment approach that

---

[105] As most companies actually do apply a gold digger mentality maybe doing the opposite makes more sense?

prevents us from keeping the strategy considerations in the board room, I recommend drawing on the insight already residing in the organization and bringing this knowledge into play as we review and refine our business models within the environment where they are and have to operate.

I recommend checking our business model environment assumptions with potential customers and partners, too. If interviews with 10-20 potential customers and partners cannot confirm our business model environment assumptions then our assumptions are most probably wrong.

EXTENDING THE BUSINESS MODEL ENVIRONMENT POTENTIAL

When we have demonstrated that our business model works and scales well with an indirect channel, then we will benefit substantially from the multitude of business model environment interpretations that our partners will perform.

A major value of the indirect channel is not only simple reach and market penetration, but also the identifications of new and different application areas that we never thought of ourselves. Our business partners will have insight into business model environments that we are not familiar with and thus they will identify business opportunities that we would never have seen. Although we have to monitor that they do not drift into areas where our product is a genuine misfit, we can benefit tremendously from the multiplier effect of the number of partners we have and the diversity they represent.

CONCLUDING BUSINESS MODEL REMARKS

This Appendix is focused on our business model - the business model of the software vendor or the principal.

Now try and build the business model of a typical independent channel partner. Compare the partner's business model with our own business model and we will see that they have very little in common.

The first big difference between our business model and the business model of our partner is in the customer value proposition area. We are product and technology focused and the channel partner is service focused. We are market focused and the channel partner is customer focused. We are working with an indirect channel approach and the channel partner is operating her channel directly. We have little relationship with the customers and the channel partner has intimate relationships with her customers. We only have revenue from our own products and the channel partner may have multiple revenue sources from multiple products and services. We need resources and activities to keep developing our products and the channel partner needs resources and activities to source, extend and manage third party products. We need resources and activities to deal with partner recruitment as well as customer engagement and the channel partner is only concerned with customer acquisition and engagement.

Our key partners are not the same. We have very few, if any, key partners where we are a key partner of our partners.

Our cost sources are completely different and one of the partners' cost streams is our entire revenue stream.

Although we may sail in the same direction we are not exactly in the same boat. We share certain common interests, but we also have objective conflicts of interest. The differences in the business models are the reason why principals and their independent channel partners often miscommunicate. We must understand our independent channel partner's business model, because we will only become successful if we can support her profitability and growth.

Figure 30: The business model and the business model environment is a great framework for discussing strategy and business development both internally and with our independent channel partners.

I recommend that you order a number of business model posters and use them to map and understand how your independent channel partners operate. Use this as your framework for communicating with your independent channel partners and you are half way to becoming successful. The remaining half comes from trying, testing and adjusting until the model works and scales.

APPENDIX C

Sample Channel Partner Agreement

OBS: THIS IS NOT A LEGAL DOCUMENT. PLEASE SEEK LEGAL ADVICE BEFORE USING THIS SAMPLE IN YOUR OPERATION.

Software Company
Street and number
Post code and city
Country
Registration number
(Hereinafter referred to as "the Software Company")

and

Business Partner
Street and number
Post code and city
Country
Registration number
(Hereinafter referred to as "Business Partner")

(Each a "party" and together referred to herein as the "parties")

Have on this [ ] day of [ ] 201[ ] (the "Effective Date") entered into the following non-exclusive business partner agreement.

PREAMBLE

Now, whereas

The Software Company wishes to ensure that the Products (as defined below) are extended, sold to and implemented with customers via an efficient and effective network of Business Partners worldwide to achieve maximum customer satisfaction and market share.

The Business Partner wishes to become part of the network of national and international Business Partners of the Software Company in order to be able to extend, supply and implement the Products to and with Customers in the Territory on a mutually non-exclusive basis, subject to the terms and conditions set out below;

Therefore, the Software Company and the Business Partner have on the Effective Date first mentioned above decided to enter into this non-exclusive Business Partner Agreement (the "Agreement").

1. DEFINITIONS

In this Agreement the following terms have the following meanings:

1. "Agreed Currency" has the meaning described in Appendix 2.

2. "Business Partner" is a reseller of the Products as defined below that has concluded an agreement with the Software Company granting the Business Partner the right to sell the licenses to use the Products, subject to fulfilling the certification requirements outlined on the Software Company's web-based Business Partner Portal.

3. "Customer" shall mean any business entity, person or other end-user (regardless of whether organized as a business entity, a not-for-profit organization or a consumer) who through the Business Partner has been licensed to use any of the Product(s). In no event shall a Customer be permitted or entitled to use the Product(s) for any other purpose than for his own use, nor shall the Customer be permitted or entitled to exploit any Product(s) commercially, regardless of whether by means of e.g. selling, letting, leasing, lending or any other means by which the Product(s) may be commercially exploited.

4. "Database" shall mean the compilation of any data supplied to the Business Partner by, or on behalf of, the Software Company or generated by the Business Partner from any such data.

5. "Group" shall mean the Software Company and its ultimate holding company and any direct or indirect subsidiary undertaking of such holding company.

6. "Intellectual Property Rights" shall mean all intellectual property rights, including patents, rights in registered and unregistered trade marks (including domain names), rights in registered and unregistered designs, trade or business names, confidential information, know-how, database rights, and copyright (including moral rights), or other industrial, intellectual or commercial rights (including rights in any invention, discovery or process), and applications for registration of any of the foregoing, and the right to apply therefore, in each case in any part of the world.

7. "Business Partner Portal" shall mean the websites established by the Software Company for the exclusive use and benefit of Business Partners, on which shall be posted e.g. information relevant to the duties and requirements of the Software Company and the Business Partners and the Customers.

8. "SCSA" shall mean the Software Company's Software Assurance, and shall cover the [mandatory or optional] subscription service provided by the Software Company for the Product(s) ensuring customers' access to support, product updates and product upgrades.

9. "Software Company Data" shall mean any data (including any personal data as defined by the [insert applicable legislation]) relating to the staff, customers or suppliers of the Software Company, documents, text, drawings, diagrams, images or sounds (together with any database made up of any of those) embodied in any medium, that are supplied to the Business Partner by, or which the Business Partner is required to generate, process, store or transmit pursuant to this Agreement.

10. "Order" Shall have the meaning ascribed to it in Article 5.1 below.

11. "Products" includes the products covered by this Agreement as specified in Appendix 1 as amended from time to time, as provided for in this Agreement.

12. "RPL" is the Reference Price List" as ascribed to it in Article 6.1 below.

13. "Territory" is the territory covered by this Agreement, which shall be strictly limited to the geographical location(s), industry or other definitions as described in Appendix 2.

2. Rights and Duties of the Business Partner

1. Subject to the terms and conditions of this Agreement the Business Partner is hereby appointed as a non-exclusive Business Partner of the Software Company in the Territory for the resale of Products and/or right-to-use (licenses) of the Products to Customers.

2. The Business Partner must offer to sell SCSA to her registered Customers on the terms and conditions applicable to such SCSA from time to time, information about which can be found on the Business Partner Portal.

3. Business Partners shall be classified in accordance with the volume of their business with the Software Company and their individual levels of competence. The structure of the classification system, levels and requirements to be met to reach the various levels as well as the benefits to which Business Partners become entitled as they progress through the classification levels may be found on the Business Partner Portal. The Software Company may change the requirements unilaterally from time to time by giving xx (XX) days advance notice to be published on the Business Partner Portal. The Business Partner must comply with all new requirements within xx (XX) days of their announcement on the Business Partner Portal. The Business Partner's classification will be reviewed annually in [month] and appropriate up- or downgrading for the coming year will become effective as of 1 [month] the same year.

4. The Business Partner shall be responsible for the resale and licensing of the Products directly to Customers in the Territory. The parties agree that all resale of the Products must be executed subject to the Software Company's standard end-user license terms and conditions in place from time to time, as further detailed in Article 15.1 below, and as available on the Business Partner Portal at any given time.

5. The Business Partner must offer technical support to his Customers according to the standards described on the Business Partner Portal at any given time.

6. In the event the Business Partner wishes to attain status as any level above "Registered Partner", the Business Partner shall be required to recruit, train and develop his staff to ensure that qualified sales and support facilities shall be available to Customers strictly in accordance with the Software Company's requirements as specified on the Business Partner Portal. In connection with the annual review of the classification of Business Partners (see Article 2.3 above) their level of certification will also be reviewed and determined for the following year, such certification to take effect from 1 [month] in any given year.

7. The Business Partner shall be required to sell the Products and/or licenses for a profit and shall set his own resale prices and shall further be required to maintain an arm's length business relationship with all his Customers. If in relation to any sale or proposed sale of Products there is any doubt or uncertainty as regards the nature of the relationship between the Business Partner and a Customer, the Business Partner must consult the Software Company in each case prior to a sale or grant of license(s) being affected.

8. Should the Business Partner wish to enter into any kind of leasing, rental or similar arrangements with a Customer concerning any Product(s), any such arrangements shall be subject to the prior approval of the Software Company. The Software Company must approve any documentation used for this purpose in advance.

9. The Business Partner may not in any way compile, decompile, recompile or disassemble the Products, reproduce, translate, amend or upgrade the underlying code or subject the Products to reverse engineering in any way except to the extent permitted by law, nor will it allow others to do so.

3. NATURE OF THE RELATIONSHIP

1. Subject to the business structure outlined above in Article 2, the Business Partner shall purchase and market the Products and licenses to the Products and sell them on arm's length terms in his own name and for his own account to Customers. The Business Partner shall act as and be deemed to be an independent trader in relation to the Software Company and any Customer(s), and neither party to this Agreement shall be deemed, for any purpose, to be an agent of the other party, and the relationship between the parties shall be that of independent contractors only.

2. The Business Partner may participate in and contribute to the marketing campaigns and sales promotions designed by Software Company and made available to promote the Products within the Territory. The Business Partner shall be expected to organize and/or implement independent sales promoting activities within the Territory in accordance with the guidelines available for such activities on the Business Partner Portal. Further information and guidelines concerning cooperation and coordination of marketing and sales promoting efforts are made available on the Business Partner Portal.

3. During the term of this Agreement the Business Partner shall establish, develop and maintain an efficient s ales a nd s ervice organization and shall at all times have all relevant functions and tasks performed only by properly skilled employees, including, but not limited to, the performance of support, service and help-desk functions in relation to the Products. The Business Partner shall maintain a staff adequate in size and expertise to sell and service the Products as well as carry out – either itself or by making appropriate arrangements with one or more other Business Partners within the Territory concerning the performance of – all relevant support and implementation obligations in relation to Products sold by him.

4. The Business Partner shall act as reseller of Software Company Products and/or licenses to Software Company Products only. All licensing relationships relating to the Products shall be strictly between Software Company and the Customers.

4. SALE AND REPORTING

1. The Business Partner shall promote the sale of the Products in the Territory at his own expense e.g. by advertising, by participating in and implementing sales promotion campaigns designed by Software Company, or by participating in and attending trade shows and exhibitions as well as by other means customary in the industry.

2. The Business Partner shall keep full records of all his activities with current and potential Customers and with other parties associated with the promotion, sales and support of the Products. This information is referred to as the Customer Database.

5. ORDERS

1. All purchase orders from the Business Partner to the Software Company shall be dated and refer to this Agreement. No additional or differing terms contained in any purchase order shall supersede or amend the terms of this Agreement, unless agreed in advance in writing and signed by both parties. Each order shall comply with and contain all relevant information required under the order procedure in force from time to time, which may be found on the Business Partner Portal. Orders must furthermore be submitted in accordance with the directions available on the Business Partner Portal. Verbal orders and instructions shall not be valid or binding on the Software Company and will not be executed.

2. All purchase orders shall be subject to acceptance by the Software Company. Time of delivery shall be stated in the Software Company's order acknowledgement.

6. PRICES

1. The purchase prices for the Products that the Business Partner purchases from the Software Company shall be the prices listed in the Reference Price List ("RPL") less an agreed discount granted to the Business Partner by the Software Company. The RPL will at all times be available on the Business Partner Portal. The margin applicable to the Business Partner will depend on his current classification (see also section 2.3 above). The classification and discount structure applied from time to time may be found on the Business Partner Portal.

2. The Software Company reserve the right unilaterally to change the RPL from time to time by giving xx (XX) days advance written notice to the Business Partner. Any open Orders received by the Software Company prior to the stipulated date for a price change will be honored at the previous RPL for a period of up to xx (XX) days after the RPL change date.

3. The Software Company shall provide the Business Partner with a reasonable number of demonstration units of the Products for the purpose of demonstrations, training and internal use by the Business Partner, the overall number of such demonstration units not to exceed xx (XX) users. Such demonstration licenses may have a time limited license code. Unless otherwise specified by the Software Company in writing, the demonstration units for standard promotional purposes will be supplied free of charge. Software upgrades for demonstration units will be provided at no cost to the Business Partner unless otherwise specified by the Software Company in writing. Any licenses for training and demonstration purposes over and beyond the above stated number provided free of charge, will be made available to the Business Partner at a discounted price, with an agreed discount of XX percent (XX%).

4. If this Agreement should expire or otherwise be terminated, the

Business Partner may purchase the relevant licenses at a price equivalent to xx percent (XX%) of the recommended retail price.

7. PAYMENTS AND DELIVERY

1. Unless otherwise agreed in writing, payment of the purchase price for the Products shall be made in the Agreed Currency and shall be due within xx (XX) calendar days of the invoice date. In the event of a delay in payment, the Business Partner shall pay interest at the rate of x% per month above the base lending rate of [name of bank], compounded quarterly, from the due payment date. The Software Company reserves the rights to withhold delivery of existing and future orders until previously dispatched and invoiced orders have been paid in full. All amounts due under this Agreement shall be paid in full without withholding of any other kind than as required by law.

2. All Products will be delivered to the Business Partner in accordance with the applicable terms of supply and delivery in force from time to time, which may be found on the Business Partner Portal.

3. The Business Partner shall be responsible for the collection, remittance and payment of any or all taxes, charges, levies, assessments and other fees of any kind imposed by any governmental or other authority on account of the acquisition, importation, sale, lease, licensing or other distribution of the Products.

4. The Products shall be delivered by the Software Company together with instruction manuals in electronic format in the languages authorized by and available from the Software Company.

8. WARRANTIES AND DISCLAIMER

1. The Products are provided to the Business Partner on an "as is" basis without warranty of any kind, express or implied, including but not limited to implied warranty of merchantability or fitness for a particular purpose. The Software Company does not represent or warrant that the Products are free from bugs or errors, or that they will operate without interruption.

2. The parties agree that the Software Company's general terms and conditions of sale and delivery in force and applicable from time to time shall also apply to all shipment(s) and all other deliveries and supplies of Products by the Software Company to the Business Partner.

9. ADVERTISING, PROMOTION AND TRAINING

1. The Business Partner may implement and promote such marketing and promotional efforts and campaigns relating to the Products as the Software Company shall make available for the purpose of influencing and working the market in the Territory, including, but not limited to, ensuring that efficient follow-up procedures and strategies are pursued vis-à-vis prospective Customers introduced to the Business Partner by the Software Company. All marketing and promotional materials will be supplied primarily in electronic form. Should the Business Partner require any promotional materials to be adapted with his logo and contact information or otherwise adjusted before publication, such adaptation(s) must comply with the advertising material guidelines available from the Business Partner Portal and must be prepared at no cost to the Software Company.

2. In order to promote and protect the image of Software Company, the Business Partner agrees to comply with the guidelines available on the Business Partner Portal concerning independently produced advertising and publicity materials.

10. Discontinued Products

1. The Software Company shall use his best efforts to provide the Business Partner with xx (XX) days prior written notice of removal of Products from the list of Products covered by this Agreement detailed in Appendix 1, as amended from time to time.

11. Prohibition Against Seeking Customers Outside the Territory

1. The Business Partner shall exercise his activities within the Territory and shall not establish branches, maintain distribution or otherwise actively seek sales or customers for the Products specified in Appendix 1 outside the Territory which are exclusively reserved by the Software Company for itself or exclusively allocated by the Software Company to other business partners. All enquiries from persons or entities outside the Territory shall be referred to the Software Company.

12. Trademarks and Symbols

1. The Business Partner shall only be entitled to use trademarks, trade names, service marks, logos or any other symbols in accordance with the design guidelines in force from time to time, which will be available on the Business Partner Portal. The Business Partner acknowledges and agrees that he has no right, title or interest in or to such trademarks, trade names, service marks, logo or other symbols except the right to use them in the manner described herein and as provided for in this Agreement. The trademarks, trade names, service marks, logo and any other symbols are and remain the registered property of Software Company and shall remain so after the expiry of this Agreement also. The Business Partner shall not without the prior written consent of Software Company register or use Internet domains using names, denominations or combinations of words similar to or likely to be confused or associated with trademarks, trade names or service marks owned by the Software Company or the Software Company Group in the Territory or elsewhere.

2. The Business Partner agrees not to register nor cause any third party to register any of the above mentioned trademarks, trade names, service marks, logo or symbols belonging to Software Company or the Software Company Group (or names or domain names similar to or likely to be confused or associated with those belonging to any company in the Software Company Group) in the Territory or elsewhere.

3. The Business Partner's right to use the Software Company's trademarks, trade names, service marks, logo or symbols as provided for under the subsections 12.1 and 12.2 above shall cease immediately on termination or expiry of this Agreement, regardless of the reason for such termination or expiry or on the written instructions of the Software Company.

4. No agreement shall be construed or interpreted as an assignment by the Software Company of any present or future Intellectual Property Rights or similar rights to the Business Partner.

13. Confidentiality and Trade Secrets

1. All commercial and/or technical information, data, specifications, drawings, other documents and software disclosed or made available to the Business Partner, as well as know-how, trade secrets or any other technical or commercial information, which the Business Partner may have in any way acquired through his activities as such (collectively "the Confidential Information") shall remain the exclusive property of the Software Company.

2. The Business Partner shall at all times treat Confidential Information with the same degree of care to avoid disclosure to any third party as is used in respect of the Business Partner's own confidential information (such care never to be less than reasonable care). The Business Partner shall in no circumstances disclose, use or otherwise make Confidential Information to any third party for any purpose other than those expressly contemplated by the Agreement.

3. After the expiry or termination of this Agreement the Business Partner shall not disclose, use or communicate Confidential Information to any third parties.

4. The Business Partner acknowledges and agrees that any breach of his obligations under this Article 13 shall cause the Software Company irreparable harm for which the Software Company shall have no adequate remedy at law. Accordingly, the Business Partner agrees that in the event of any such breach, the Software Company shall be entitled to seek and obtain a temporary restraining order, preliminary and permanent injunctive relief and/or an order for specific performance to protect its rights and interests in and to the Confidential Information.

14 Unfair Competition and Infringements

1. The Business Partner shall inform the Software Company of all acts of unfair competition affecting the Products or the Software Company and of all infringements of the industrial and intellectual property rights of the Software Company that come to his notice, and it shall assist the Software Company to the best of his ability in protecting the Software Company against such acts and infringements.

2. The Software Company agrees to defend the Business Partner against, or at the Software Company's option, settle, any lawsuit, claim or other legal action brought against the Business Partner alleging that the Business Partner's use of the Products infringes any patent, trademark or trade secret, or other intellectual property right always provided that the Business Partner shall have promptly advised the Software Company of any such lawsuit, claim or action, and further provided that the Business Partner co-operates with the Software Company in the defense and settlement thereof. The Software Company shall have exclusive control of the defense against such actions and of all negotiations for settlement or compromise thereof. This Article shall not apply to actions arising from (i) the combination, operation or use of any Products supplied hereunder with products, software or data not supplied by the Software Company, or (ii) any use of the Products in a manner, place or circumstances not contemplated hereby.

15. STANDARD END-USER LICENSE CERTIFICATE

1. Each Product shall be provided with Software Company's standard end-user license certificate in place from time to time. The Business Partner warrants that all Products sold or licensed to Customers by the Business Partner shall be sold subject to the terms and conditions of Software Company's standard end-user license certificate in place from time to time available on the Business Partner Portal (attached hereto as Appendix 3 in the version in force on the Effective Date of this Agreement).

16. ASSIGNMENT

1. The Software Company shall be free to assign this Agreement and all rights and obligations hereunder to any third party at any time.

2. The Business Partner may only assign this Agreement and his rights and obligations hereunder to a third party provided the Software Company's prior written consent has been obtained.

17. TERMINATION

1. Either party giving x (X) months written notice by registered post to the other party for the Agreement to terminate at the end of [insert time] may terminate this Agreement.

18. EARLY TERMINATION

1. This Agreement may be terminated immediately by either party by sending written notice to the other party by registered mail in the event of a material breach of the terms of this Agreement by either party, where the breaching party fails to rectify such breach within xx (XX) days after receipt of written notice of such breach from the other party.

2. The Software Company may terminate this Agreement immediately by the Software Company by sending written notice to the Business Partner in the event of either of the following events occurring:

> **2.1.** The dissolution or liquidation of the Business Partner, her bankruptcy, her suspension of payment, the entry into any voluntary composition with her creditors, the attachment of her assets for the benefit of creditors, or other analogous events; and/or

> **2.2.** The change of the legal structure, control over or ownership of the Business Partner.

19. AFTER TERMINATION

1. Upon the expiry or termination of this Agreement, the Business Partner shall immediately return to the Software Company, at no cost to the Software Company, all Product information and Product related materials in his possession.

2. The Software Company shall not be bound to accept the return of any Products from the Business Partner's stock on the expiry or termination of this Agreement. In the event of termination of the Agreement, the Business Partner expressly agrees to refrain from selling the Products in stock at reduced prices within or outside the Territory.

3. Upon the termination of this Agreement, for whatever reason, the Business Partner must provide an electronic copy of the fully updated Customer Database (see Article 4.2 above) to the Software Company within xx (XX) days of termination. In the event the Business Partner is unable to ensure that her Customers at the time of the termination will continue to receive the same level of support in relation to the Products as defined on the Business Partner Portal at any given time, the Software Company shall be entitled to unilaterally assign all such Customers to other business partners in the Territory. The Business Partner shall not be entitled to compensation or damages on account of such an assignment.

4. Provided the Agreement has been terminated for reasons other than the Business Partner's material breach of his obligations under this Agreement, the Software Company will agree, for a period of xx (XX) days from date of termination or expiry and subject to article 5.2 hereof, to execute orders filed and accepted prior to the expiry or termination date.

20. Indemnities and Compensation

1. No claims for indemnity or compensation can be lodged on account of the expiry or termination of this Agreement, save where these claims are based on the material breach of this Agreement by one of the parties or on mandatory regulations.

21. LIMITATION OF LIABILITY

1. The Business Partner shall indemnify and hold the Software Company harmless from any liability and expenses arising out of or in connection with any claim, action, suit, demands or expenses incurred by the Software Company resulting from (i) distribution of Products by the Business Partner, its officers, e mployees o r agents or (ii) any breach of this Agreement by the Business Partner, its officers, employees or agents.

2. The exclusions and limitations of liability contained in this Agreement shall apply regardless of whether the loss or damage was foreseeable or whether the Business Partner notifies the Software Company of the possibility of any greater loss or damage, but shall not apply to the extent prohibited or limited by law and, in particular, nothing in this Agreement shall affect the liability of either party for death or personal injury caused by negligence or for fraudulent misrepresentation or other fraud.

3. The liability in aggregate of the Software Company for loss or damage to tangible property of the Business Partner caused by his negligence shall not exceed [insert amount].

4. Except as provided above, the liability of the Software Company for a claim made by the Business Partner in respect of loss or damage suffered by the Business Partner under this Agreement flowing from any one event or series of connected events shall not exceed the higher of the purchase price for the Product(s) giving rise to the liability or [insert amount] however arising.

5. The term "however arising" covers all causes and actions giving rise to liability of the Software Company arising out of or in connection with the Agreement and/or the Products (i) whether arising by reason of any misrepresentation (whether made prior to and/or in the Agreement or after it entry) negligence or other tort, breach of statutory duty, renunciation, repudiation or other breach of contract, restitution or otherwise; (ii) whether arising under an indemnity; (iii) whether caused by any total or partial delay in the supply of the Products or defective Products; and (iv) whether deliberate (but not with malicious intent) or otherwise, however, fundamental the result.

6. The Software Company shall not be liable to the Business Partner for any loss of profit, production, anticipated savings, goodwill or business opportunities or any type of indirect, economic or consequential loss even if that loss or damage was reasonably foreseeable or the Software Company was aware of the possibility of that loss or damage arising.

7. To the extent determined from time to time by the Software Company, each of the members of the Software Company's Group and the employees of the Software Company and such members shall be entitled to benefit from every indemnity and exclusion and limitation of liability expressed in favor of the Software Company, so that the liability of all of them and the Software Company in total shall be no greater than the liability of the Software Company alone as set out in this Agreement. No third party's consent shall be required to cancel or vary the Agreement.

8. In no circumstances shall the Software Company have any liability whatsoever to the Business Partner for any claims, whether for damages or other compensation, resulting from, arising out of or in connection with the Business Partner's sale of Products to Costumers and/or Consumers.

22. FORCE MAJEURE

1. Neither party shall be liable for any failure to perform her obligations hereunder (except timely payment of monies due) due to events or circumstances outside her reasonable control, including but not limited to fire, explosion, flood, lightning, Acts of God, acts of terrorism, war, rebellion, riot or other civil disorder, sabotage, orders or requests by any Government or any other authority, strikes, lockouts or other labor disputes (but not those including the Business Partner's own workforce), but each party shall use her best endeavors to minimize the consequences or losses to the other party as a consequence of such events.

23. GOVERNING LAW AND LEGAL VENUE

1. This Agreement and any matters arising out of or relating to it shall be governed by and construed in accordance with the laws of [insert place]

2. Any dispute, controversy or claim arising out of or in connection with this Agreement or the breach, termination or validity hereof shall be finally settled by arbitration in accordance with the Arbitration Rules of the [insert venue].

3. The language of the arbitration shall be [language].

4. Any dispute, controversy or claim arising out of or relating to this Agreement including but not limited to the possibility or existence of the proceedings, the proceedings themselves, oral statements made during the course of the proceedings, documents and other information submitted by the parties or prepared by the court or the arbitrator(s), and the final award shall be deemed Confidential Information under Article 13 of this Agreement.

5. Notwithstanding the aforementioned, the Software Company shall not be precluded from bringing an action in any court of competent jurisdiction for injunctive or other provisional relief or for the collection of undisputed outstanding accounts. Nothing in this Agreement shall be deemed to limit the parties' rights to seek interim injunctive relief or to enforce an arbitration award in any court of law.

24. MISCELLANEOUS

1. The terms and provisions included in this Agreement constitute the entire agreement between the parties and supersede all previous communications, representations, agreements, or understanding, whether oral or written, between the parties concerning the subject matter of this Agreement.

2. With the exception of Appendices 1-3, which can be unilaterally changed by the Software Company, all modifications and amendments to this Agreement must be agreed in writing and signed by both parties.

3. The provisions of this Agreement shall be severable. In the event that any provision of this Agreement is found to be invalid, illegal or unenforceable, such finding shall not affect the validity and enforceability of any of the remaining provisions of this Agreement. If any part of this Agreement becomes invalid, illegal or unenforceable the parties shall negotiate in good faith in order to agree the terms of a mutually satisfactory replacement for such invalid, illegal or unenforceable provision which as closely as possible reflects their intentions as expressed in this Agreement and validly gives effect thereto. Failure to agree on a replacement provision within six (6) months of commencing such negotiations shall result in the automatic termination of this Agreement. The obligations of the parties pursuant to any invalid, illegal or unenforceable provision of the Agreement shall be suspended during such negotiations.

4. No failure by a party to pursue any remedy resulting from a breach by the other party of this Agreement shall be construed as a waiver of that breach by the former party or as a waiver of any subsequent or other breach.

5. All provisions that by their nature survive the expiry or termination of this Agreement shall remain in full force and effect after its expiry or termination.

6. The Appendices attached hereto form an integral part of this Agreement. In the event of any discrepancy between any provisions in the Appendices and this document, the provisions of this Agreement shall prevail.

7. It is an express condition of this Agreement that, for the duration of this Agreement, or for a period of twelve months after its termination for whatever reason, neither party shall, under any circumstances whether alone or jointly, with or on behalf of another and whether directly or indirectly employ or make offers of employment to or offer to conclude any contract for services with any individual who is or was at any time within the previous 6 months an employee of the other party in a senior position (including all officers, managers, sales persons or developers).

8. If either party breaches clause 24.7.1 the parties agree to liquidated damages and that party shall be liable in the amount of one third of the current annual salary previously paid by the other in respect of the relevant employee.

9. The provisions of this clause 24 shall survive the termination, for whatever reason, of this Agreement.

APPENDICES

Appendices, forming an integral part of the Agreement

1. **Appendix 1 – List of Products**
2. **Appendix 2 – Territory and Agreed Currency**
3. **Appendix 3 – The Software Company's Standard**

License Terms (subject to updating from time to time)

Appendix D

The Channel Partner P&L

The dynamics of channel partner recruitment fundamentally change as we grow from early mode to mature mode. In early mode we have to invest substantial effort every time we recruit an individual channel partner and if the partner fails to take off we have lost time and money. The channel partner P&L is an important tool in the process for finding and qualifying the partners that are serious about building a business around our product.

The channel partner P&L is the quantitative outcome of the business model and the business model environment analysis represents the revenue, CoGS[106], CapEx[107] and OpEx[108] consequences of the activities associated with executing our joint business plan.

---

[106] Cost of Goods Sold

[107] Capital Expenditure from investments

[108] Operational Expenses

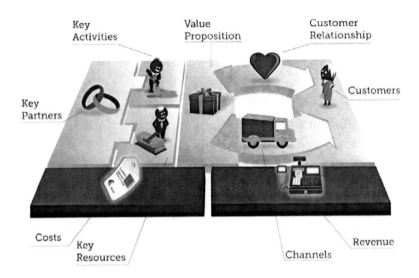

Figure 32: The channel partner P&L is the quantitative financial result of our decisions on how to start and build a business around our product.

The conclusion of the strategy workshop should be an action plan and a corresponding budget and as each individual channel partner represents a unique scenario defined by her current customer base, organizational capabilities and financial strength the plans and budgets will never be identical for any two partners.

We therefore develop an ideal channel partner business model with a certain minimum organizational setup and with a certain set of activities that we know[109] will generate a certain volume of business within a certain timeframe. Without this business model template we will have a hard time assessing if the potential channel partner is

---

[109] We may not exactly know the relationship between investment in activities and the resulting revenue and gross margin outcome, but we can either refer to a model specifying the assumptions or refer to empirical material from our current operations.

really committed to investing in the business and the channel partner will have a hard time assessing if we have any idea about what it takes to build a business with our own product. The actual business model and P&L of each channel partner will always be individual given the specific scenarios.

As indicated in figure 33 the P&L has a revenue and a cost section. Where do we start? I suggest we follow this sequence:

Value Proposition ▸ Customer Segments ▸ Activities ▸ Resources ▸ OpEx and CapEx ▸ Revenue ▸ CoGS ▸ P&L

We will have standard templates for each of the business model building blocks, but as we review the individual channel partner scenario we will adjust them together with the partner's management team until we have a version that they can assume ownership of.

Many independent channel partners have never undertaken such exercises before and we therefore need to provide quite detailed templates and tutorials on the various parts of the process.

1.000 EUR	Q1	Q2	Q3	Q4	Q1	Q2	Q3	Q4	Q1	Q2	Q3	Q4
Revenue												
License revenue	0	0	100	200	100	200	315	315	330	330	360	660
License maintenance	0	0	0	0	0	0	17	17	34	34	51	51
Service revenue	0	0	100	200	100	200	315	315	315	300	300	630
Total revenue	0	0	200	400	200	400	647	647	679	664	711	1.341
Cost of Goods Sold												
License revenue	0	0	60	120	60	120	189	189	198	198	216	396
License maintenance	0	0	0	0	0	0	14	14	27	27	41	41
Service revenue	0	0	60	120	60	120	189	189	189	180	180	378
Total COGS	0	0	120	240	120	240	392	392	414	405	437	815
Gross Margin	0	0	80	160	80	160	255	255	265	259	274	526
Operating Expenses (OPEX)												
Marketing	9	9	9	9	19	19	19	19	25	25	25	25
Sales expenses	20	40	60	60	58	90	105	105	88	89	144	180
Management overhead	11	4	6	6	5	7	8	8	4	4	7	9
Initial training	30	10	1	0	0	0	0	0	0	0	0	0
Total operating expenses	70	63	76	75	81	116	132	132	117	118	176	214
P&L	-70	-63	4	85	-1	44	123	123	147	140	98	312
Accumulated Profit	-70	-133	-128	-43	-44	0	123	247	394	534	632	945
	Q1	Q2	Q3	Q4	Q1	Q2	Q3	Q4	Q1	Q2	Q3	Q4
Accumulated Gross Profit	0	0	80	240	320	480	735	991	1.256	1.514	1.789	2.315
Accumulated OPEX	70	133	208	283	364	480	612	744	862	980	1.156	1.370
Cash Flow	-70	-63	-76	5	79	-36	28	123	138	146	83	60
Accumulate cash flow	-70	-133	-208	-203	-124	-160	-132	-9	129	276	358	413

Figure 33: A P&L for a business with an average sales cycle of 5 months and an average order size of €100,000. Behind each line in the P&L is a detailed set of assumptions in terms of activities and resources.

The P&L shown in figure 33 yields an accumulated profit of almost €1 million over the first 3 years, requires a cash injection of around €210.000 and is an excellent business case. Without such a scenario most independent channel partners will focus entirely on the investments required in the first 12-month period, and getting a business with a value proposition with an average sales cycle of 5 months off the ground will never be profitable in the first year.

Assumptions	Units	Number	Comment
Average license order	EUR	100.000	
Average Service order	EUR	100.000	
License add-on	Per year	15%	From year 2
Service add-on	Per year	15%	From year 2
Software maintenance	Per year	17%	From year 2
Margin on license orders		40%	
Margin on Services		40%	
Margin of software maintenance		20%	
Average sales cycle	Months	8	Year 1
Average sales cycle	Months	6	Year 2
Average sales cycle	Months	5	Year 3
Average sales cost in percentage of revenue	20%	2,5%	Year 1
Average sales cost in percentage of revenue	18%	2,9%	Year 2
Average sales cost in percentage of revenue	15%	3,0%	Year 3
Average sales cost in percentage of revenue	20%	2,5%	Year 1
Average sales cost in percentage of revenue	18%	2,9%	Year 2
Average sales cost in percentage of revenue	15%	3,0%	Year 3
Management overhead	Of sales	10%	Year 1
		8%	Year 2
		5%	Year 3
Initial training package	EUR	15.000	
Marketing	EUR	35.000	Year 1
	EUR	75.000	Year 2
	EUR	100.000	Year 3

Figure 34: General P&L scenario assumptions.

The general assumptions behind the P&L scenario we describe in this Appendix operate with an 8-months sales cycle in the first twelve months, a 6-months sales cycle in the following twelve months, reaching the average 5-months sales cycle in the last twelve month period. There may be specific reasons for reducing the sales cycle expectation, but in general there is always a learning curve that we have to overcome before a new channel partner can produce the same productivity as our more experienced channel partners.

We also assume that the customer acquisition cost in general is higher in the beginning and that there is a need for more management attention when we commence the project. Supporting our business case we need a best practice sales process explaining the steps we recommend that she takes to find, win, make, keep and grow happy customers, including the marketing investments required and the conversion rates we expect for the various stages of the sales process.

As we work our way through the business model and the corresponding P&L we will realize that the channel partner will benefit dramatically from selling to her installed base of customers first. If that, for some reason, is not possible then a big red flag should be assigned to the business case, because selling a new product through a new channel partner to new customers is a green-field operation. There may be situations where this scenario is perfectly adequate, but in most situations it will not fly without major investment, management attention and patience.

When we have our action plan and budget in place then we have to define the KPIs that we need to monitor as we enter the execution stage. Even the best thought-out plan will not survive intercepting with reality. Without the KPIs we will not be able to identify what is deviating from our assumptions, and we will end up in useless discussions exchanging "opinions" about what went wrong and what we need to do to get back on track.

Software companies that have no or only limited experience selling their own products will obviously have a hard time putting together a business model and P&L scenario based on hard facts representing some statistical significance, but that doesn't mean that we should do nothing and come empty handed to the strategy workshop table with the channel partners. When we have little experience or are moving into new markets with different business model environments, then we need to work closely together with our channel partners learning what the best practices are and what the conversion rates are to build scenarios that we can use to help ramp up future channel partners.

APPENDIX E

SOCIAL MEDIA MARKETING AND SALES: POETS, PLUMBERS AND THE DEATH OF PROPAGANDA

There many more books on social media marketing than there are books on building successful partner channels. We should definitely read some of the first, because ignoring social media is to miss an opportunity to engage with our potential customer exactly where they spend an awful lot of time searching for information and inspiration. Nevertheless, I see many software companies failing to support their channel partners in this area and I have therefore included some basic recommendations in this Appendix.

Before the invention of the Internet, marketing communication was a well-defined profession in terms of messaging, channels and production options. I am not saying that marketing was easy and predictable I am just saying that crafting the messages, choosing the channels and production were well-defined disciplines supported by a mature and well-organized industry.

Today we must face the fact that our customers and influential stakeholders spend far more time on the web, and especially in front of social media, than they spend watching, reading and listening to content delivered through the pre-Internet channels such as broadcast-TV, radio, magazines and newspapers. We can also conclude that they are influenced by many more information channels, types and sources than was the case just 15 years ago and that these channels, types and sources are constantly changing. And we can conclude that the level of noise is enormous and steadily increasing.

Just as we were providing marketing and sales support before the Internet with templates for direct mails, call scripts, advertisements, seminars, brochures, testimonials etc. we also need to help our channel partners to reach our target customers and influential stakeholders on the web, and I have developed a simple model that can support our efforts.

FIRST THINGS FIRST

Before we dive into buying Adwords campaigns, banner ads and sponsored content on the web and on social media we need to do our homework first. Fortunately this is also a result of the business model and business model environment analysis we perform prior to defining our other plans and budgets.

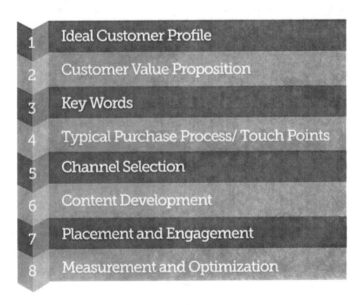

1 Ideal Customer Profile
2 Customer Value Proposition
3 Key Words
4 Typical Purchase Process/ Touch Points
5 Channel Selection
6 Content Development
7 Placement and Engagement
8 Measurement and Optimization

Figure 35: A simple model for marketing and sales operations on the web and on social media.

Step 1: Doing anything meaningful in marketing first and foremost requires that we know which target segment we want to communicate with. We need to nail the definition of the ideal customer profile because on the web and specifically on the social media platforms we always should direct our messages to our target audience.

Step 2: The next thing we need to have defined is our customer value proposition, to help us identify what is it that we eventually want our target audience to buy from us. With our core deliveries in mind we can now identify the areas where we should build our reputation as specialists or thought leaders.

Step 3: Define our keywords. What are the key words or key phrases that our potential customers will use when searching for information on the things that we provide? Without the keywords/phrases we will be roaming blindly on the web and on the social media. There are people and tools available to help us define our keywords/phrases and I urge you to have access to this expertise either internally or externally. Getting the keywords/phrases identified is critical to the success of our activities on the web.

Step 4: Define the customer journey, or the typical customer purchase process, including the touch points where we expect to engage with our potential customers. For each touch point we will have to define an engagement strategy. Smaller companies may identify just a handful of touch points, but no one can afford to completely ignore the customer journey.

Step 5: Select the channels where we will engage with our target audience. The web offers thousands of channels and there is no way we can communicate on them all. We will need to identify those where we can engage most cost-effectively. In the good old days we went to the media people to choose the best mix of channels for a given campaign and this is no different today. There are people who make a living from knowing the characteristics of the channels available to us and we should consult them before we choose our mix.

Step 6: Develop the content that we will make available in the touch points. I will discuss the role of content below, but here I will emphasize that this step appears to be the most difficult for software companies as well as their channel partners. Leaving content development only to the channel partners is not an option if we want to engage effectively with our target customers and key influential stakeholders on the web.

Step 7: Placement and engagement. This can be compared to running a classified advert in the local newspaper, placing a display advert in a magazine, getting a piece of PR into a news media, sending a direct mail or making a phone call, but there are some profound differences when operating on the web where many of the activities can be interconnected, responses individualized and automated, and the impact measured.

To help us decide placement and engagement we must answer four basic questions:

+ Where and how do potential customers, that need what we have, find us?

+ Where and how can we find potential customers that need what we have?

+ How do we motivate to engagement (call-to-action) when we meet?

+ Which of the combinations of channels/messages/engagement are most cost effective?

As no one can answer these questions up front we need to have a **Step 8** where we measure the performance (reach and conversion rates) of the channels/messages/engagement combinations, test new combinations and continuously optimize the process. Using the web and social media to support our customer acquisition process is very much a trial and error process.

POETS & PLUMBERS

Operating successfully on the web requires mastering a large portfolio of skills that I have yet to see represented in a single individual. Let me list some of the competences and skills required:

- Marketing strategy defining customer value propositions and ideal customer profiles
- Domain experience and insight in the areas where we are to build authority and thought leadership
- Designing customer journeys and corresponding engagement strategies
- Crafting quality textual content
- Designing communicative illustrations
- Understanding the characteristics of the various web channels
- Understanding the operational details of the individual channels
- Understanding the tools available for operating across channels
- Programming skills reformatting the designers proposals to formats presentable in the various browser and device formats
- Understanding the analytics tools, analyzing the performance of our activities and proposing optimization opportunities
- Project management and coordination
- People management and leadership

Communicating on the web may seem inexpensive at first glance, but that is only the case when we have no objectives and are happy with random results. If we want to engage systematically with our potential customers on the web, which is where they spend an awful lot of time, then we need to make investments, engage resources and systematically perform activities. A vast majority of our independent channel partners cannot and will not do a professional job on web and social media marketing and without our assistance and contribution we are missing a huge opportunity in supporting the process of finding, winning, making, keeping and growing happy customers.

THE DEATH OF PROPAGANDA

You have probably heard the term "content marketing," which means that we move the focus of our communication from praising ourselves and our products to discussing the challenges facing our customers and how we can inspire and help them find solutions. Communication where we promote and praise ourselves is called propaganda[110] and propaganda is not only dead it is counter-productive. It doesn't mean that we cannot talk about who we are and what we do, but such content should only be available upon request when our key audiences have read, heard or watched our contributions to how they can improve their businesses.

PRODUCING QUALITY CONTENT IS DIFFICULT

Producing quality content is much more difficult (and e xpensive) than producing propaganda, and by leaving the job to the individual independent channel partner we will be missing out on an obvious economy of scale opportunity. Where propaganda production is something we do from time to time, content production is an ongoing effort requiring domain experience and insight in the areas where we are to build authority and thought leadership. However, quality content can be reformatted and reused on many channels and when

---

[110] This issue is thoroughly discussed in the recommended book: Jonathan Winch, Michael Best, and David Hoskins. 2011. The death of propaganda : B2B buyer behavior has changed - now it's your turn (Eye for Image: Copenhagen).

re-communicated and endorsed it can reach large audiences.

I recommend software companies running indirect channels to take charge and lead the production on quality content that the partners can share, but I also recommend that we invest in helping the channel partners contribute to the production of content that we can share and recommend to other partners.

SOCIAL MEDIA ORCHESTRATION

As the vendor operating a partner channel we must take charge and "lead" the effort associated with communicating and engaging with our potential customers on the web.

I will recommend a simple format for helping our channel partners include the web in their marketing and sales activities.

Figure 36: A simple format to help our channel partners include the web and social media in their marketing and sale activities.

Step1: Before we start taking the lead we need to get our own marketing strategy and plans communicated, allowing the partners to leverage from what we do. We therefore need to communicate our plans and what the channel partners can expect from us.

Step 2: Building a repository of content that our channel partners can reuse on their chosen communication channels and in the engagement points that we have decided to support is fundamental. We should reach out to our channel partners and identify quality content that we can help reformat and repurpose for communication across our partner channel.

Step 3: Organize training and workshops where the channel partners can learn about web and social media communication "best practice" specifically related to our domain. Working together will require a certain level of competence in this field.

Step 4: Build and maintain a list of recommended vendors who understand our own marketing strategies and the domain in which we operate. I am not recommending a formalized certification process, but rather suggesting a very loose network of service providers that the channel partners can choose to work with knowing that the domain related leaning curve is somewhat short. Only very big companies can justify having all the resources needed for running effective web based marketing and sales activities in-house and nursing a large group of service providers will help our channel partners engage such resources as required.

APPENDIX F

EXCLUSIVITY

Independent channel partners in general have a bilateral non-exclusive right to sell our products to her customers. Bilateral means that we can freely appoint other resellers selling the same product to the same customers and that the channel partner can likewise choose to sell competitive products alongside our product. In the early mode stage of developing our indirect channel we will often be met with a request for some sort of exclusivity as the channel partner, that we are about to recruit, wants to protect her investments in the engagement with us.

As discussed in chapter 10, exclusive arrangements are not unusual when appointing distributors that invest in brand promotion and channel development on our behalf as it would be very difficult to motivate anybody to invest in such activities knowing that we may appoint another channel partner tomorrow that would benefit from a free ride on these investments.

Granting someone an exclusive right is a limitation of our future options and should never be given without reasonable compensation and in most cases such compensation is a firm purchase commitment. I often see software companies grant exclusive rights to channel partners operating in non-core territories, probably because they consider not having any opportunity cost in such a situation. I urge you to be cautious as exclusivity often has the exact opposite effect making the channel partner lean back, do nothing or very little and then picking up on inbound inquiries only generated by spill-over from our sales and marketing activities in other territories.

Dealing with the exclusivity question I therefore recommend to distinguishing between "de jure" exclusivity and "de facto" exclusivity.

DE JURE EXCLUSIVITY

When we make the decision to sell though independent channel partners we are entering a business practice that is regulated by law in most countries, as governments don't like agreements aimed at limiting free competition. If we agree to grant de jure exclusivity to a channel partner then we must consider the following issues over and above the usual terms and conditions for a business partner agreement:

1. How do we formulate the exclusivity and also comply with the legal requirements for the territory?

2. What firm commitments do we get in return for the exclusivity?

3. Where does the exclusivity apply and what does that imply in terms of the channel partner's operation outside the agreed territory or domain?

4. How does the exclusivity with this channel partner impact the agreements we make with other channel partners?

5. What happens if and when we terminate the exclusivity?

As previously mentioned, exclusivity is mostly an issue for distributors who make major market development investments on our behalf. Exclusive rights are typically out of the question for channel partners serving the final customers and where her market penetration capability is only a small fraction of what we need to achieve market leadership. Granting formal exclusive rights should always be reciprocated with firm commitments as opposed to only sincere intentions and best effort.

DE FACTO EXCLUSIVITY

There may be situations where we will give a channel partner a head start and protect her investment in a certain limited time period where she can demonstrate the capability to actually deliver on her promises, but without her having any firm commitments to fulfill. In this situation we will sign a standard non-exclusive agreement and then give the channel partner a more informal and often short-term protection that expires on a certain day, that we can withdraw if the business doesn't develop as we expected or if our options suddenly change. It is easier for us to make an informal gentleman's agreement under a certain set of assumptions, than it is to develop and sign a formal exclusive agreement, which requires a lot of preparation and consideration.

Oral agreements should obviously be honored exactly as written agreements and the agreements we make outside the formal channel partner agreement should be no less precise and binding. When a channel partner has no firm commitments to deliver against and the business develops in a different way from what we both expected, then we are in a better position to return to the negotiation table to review the situation.

As we build our network of channel partners there will often be situations where we make no formal commitments or promises of protection, but where we nevertheless do not actively recruit competing channel partners. If our territory is not yet saturated, then we will benefit from recruiting channel partners that are not actively competing with each other with their outbound activities. Applying the "we currently have no plans..." approach can actually be very helpful for some channel partners in getting a head start in a certain location or domain without them having to make firm commitments.

APPENDIX G

LITERATURE

Treacy, M., & Wiersema, F. D. (1995). The discipline of market leaders: choose your customers, narrow your focus, dominate your market. Reading, Mass.: Addison-Wesley Pub. Co.

Gladwell, M. (2002). The tipping point : how little things can make a big difference (1st Back Bay pbk. ed.). Boston: Back Bay Books.

Osterwalder, A., Pigneur, Y., & Clark, T. (2010). Business model generation: a handbook for visionaries, game changers, and challengers. Hoboken, NJ: Wiley.

Winch, J., Best, M., & Hoskins, D. (2011). The death of propaganda: B2B buyer behavior has changed - now it's your turn. Copenhagen: Eye for Image.

Wood, J. B., Hewlin, T., & Lah, T. E. (2011). Consumption economics: the new rules of tech. California: Point B Inc.

Blank, S. D., Bob. (2012). The startup owner's manual: the step-by-step guide for building a great company (1 ed.): K & S Ranch.

Roberge, Mark (2015). The sales acceleration formula: using data, technology, and inbound selling to go from $0 to $100 million. Hoboken, New Jersey: John Wiley & Sons, Inc.

Bech, H. P. (2013). Entering foreign markets in the software industry - the BECH Index 2013. Copenhagen, Denmark: TBK Publishing®.

Bech, H. P. (2013). Business model generation – the emperor's new clothes? Copenhagen, Denmark: TBK Publishing®.

Bech, H. P. (2013). Channel partner recruitment in the software industry. Copenhagen, Denmark: TBK Publishing®.

Bech, H. P. (2013). Managing a reseller channel in the software industry. Copenhagen, Denmark: TBK Publishing®.

Bech, H. P. (2013). Growth through partners (the path to market dominance through a channel of partners in the software industry). Copenhagen, Denmark: TBK Publishing®.

Bech, H. P. (2013). The software partner channel and the customer value propositions. Copenhagen, Denmark: TBK Publishing®.

Bech, H. P. (2013). The software partner channel in a business model context. Copenhagen, Denmark: TBK Publishing®.

Bech, H. P. (2014). The partner P&L – a key to building successful channel partners in the software industry. Copenhagen, Denmark: TBK Publishing®.

Bech, H. P. (2014). Designing effective channel partner programs in the software industry. Copenhagen, Denmark: TBK Publishing®.

Bech, H. P. (2014). Commonly used definitions in the software industry front office. Copenhagen, Denmark: TBK Publishing®.

Bech, H. P. (2014). The value chain & AIDA process in the software industry. Copenhagen, Denmark: TBK Publishing®.

Moore, G. A. (2014). Crossing the chasm : marketing and selling disruptive products to mainstream customers (third edition ed.). New York, NY: HarperBusiness, an imprint of HarperCollins Publishers.

Osterwalder, A., Pigneur, Y., Bernarda, G., & Smith, A. (2014). Value proposition design: how to create products and services customers want.

Bech, H. P. (2015). Building successful partner channels: the business model in the business model. Copenhagen, Denmark: TBK Publishing®.

OTHER BOOKS BY THE AUTHOR

Bech, Hans Peter. 2012. Strategic planning and budgeting guidelines for independent software vendors (TBK Publishing®: Copenhagen, Denmark).

Bech, Hans Peter. 2013. Management consulting essentials (TBK Publishing®: Copenhagen, Denmark).

APPENDIX H

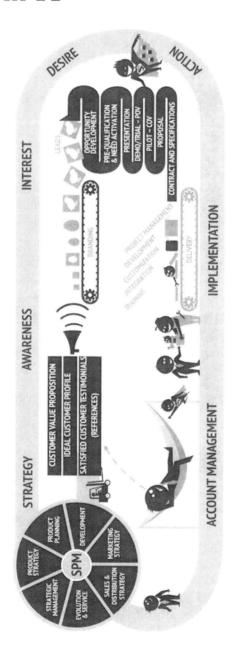

Software Industry Value Chain

ABOUT THE AUTHOR

After graduating with an M.Sc. (Econ) degree from the University of Copenhagen in 1977, Hans Peter worked as a civil servant for the Ministry of Employment in the department for economic and statistical analysis.

In 1980 he was recruited as a sales trainee by Control Data Corporation (Minneapolis, Minnesota, USA) and went through an extensive 2-year training program after which he was assigned to large corporate accounts as a salesman of computer mainframes and customized software development projects. In 1982 he made it to his first 100% Club and in 1983 he qualified for the Control Data Summit Conference, which was reserved for the top performing sales people worldwide. In 1984 Hans Peter was promoted to sales manger and made responsible for all new business development initiatives such as e-learning (PLATO), CAD/CAM (ICEM), Cybernet (an early attempt to create the Internet), LAN/WAN solutions and on-line trading platforms (early version of e-commerce).

In 1986 he was recruited by a Danish start-up (Dataco) to lead the revenue generating activities for their new line of LAN and WAN products based on the open ISO-OSI protocol stack. Dataco became a huge success and within a few years Hans Peter had established a network of resellers across Europe and initiated OEM activities in the

USA. In 1988 he was recruited by another Danish start-up (Mercante) to repeat the Dataco success, which he did and within twelve months a high performing reseller network was established across Europe, an OEM deal was closed with XEROX in the US and several other OEM deals were in the pipeline. Unfortunately the company suffered from severe product quality issues, filed for bankruptcy in 1989 and Hans Peter Bech accepted an invitation to become the country manager for Data General in Denmark.

In 1992 he returned to work with internationalization projects for the Danish software industry and was made responsible for software revenue generation worldwide for Dansk Data Elektronik (DDE). For three years he traveled the world building relationships with media executives promoting EUROMAX, which was a completely new approach for managing the entire production (editorial, advertisement and production) of newspapers. Due to strategy disagreements with the management at DDE, Hans Peter left the company and agreed to join RE Technology in 1995. After the merger of RE and BARCO in 1997 he was recruited by Damgaard Data to join the team responsible for taking over worldwide distribution from IBM.

In 1998 Hans Peter moved to Stuttgart with his family and spent three years building the channel partner network for Concorde XAL (now Microsoft Dynamics XAL) and AXAPTA (now Microsoft Dynamics AX) in Germany, Austria and Switzerland. After the merger between Damgaard Data and Navision Software Hans Peter was promoted to Vice President for Central Europe and headed the merger of the operations in Germany, Austria, Switzerland, The Netherlands, Belgium, Poland, Slovenia and Russia.

In 2000 Hans Peter was highlighted by Computerworld Denmark as one of the 100 most influential people in the Danish IT industry. In 2001 he returned to Denmark to start his own business and was active in several startups and turnarounds as a business angel.

Together with his long time friend Gianmaria Odello[111] he founded TBK Consult in 2007. TBK Consult is a global network of independent management consultants helping their software industry clients with revenue growth and in particular global market penetration. In 2010 Hans Peter founded TBK Publishing®, which publishes books, white papers and other publications focused on business development in the software industry. In 2013 he founded TBK Academy® that facilitates strategy and business development workshops for software industry executives.

In 2014 the Executive Development Unit of the Sabanci University in Istanbul, Turkey invited Hans Peter to run a series of workshops for the TETSoft Software Clusters, which is an activity in Turkish Government's UR-GE sectorial program for industrial development organized by IMMIB[112] and sponsored by the Ministry of Economy.

As a management consultant and workshop facilitator Hans Peter has been involved with numerous international business development projects in the software industry and among his clients are companies such as Microsoft, Danfoss, Secunia, XINK, SoftScan, EG, Jabra, Milestone Systems, Targit, Jeeves, Natek, Netop Business Solutions, Workcube, CSC Scandihealth, Blancco and many, many more.

Hans Peter divides his time between writing articles and books on business development in the software industry, facilitating executive workshops, giving keynote speeches and providing management consulting for selected clients.

He has also served as a non-executive board member for companies such as The Peerless Factories, Cursum (e-learning) and SMT Data. Hans Peter enjoys traveling, skiing, hiking and biking and he plays guitar and is the lead singer in two amateur bands. He is married to Sue, has two children and five grandchildren.

---

[111] Gianmaria passed away on March 4th 2015. We will miss him, but his integrity and passion will stay as an inspiration for all of us.

[112] Istanbul Minerals & Metals Exporters' Associations

CPSIA information can be obtained at www.ICGtesting.com
Printed in the USA
LVOW07s1004161015

458554LV00014B/311/P